With Australia as her case study, Gomes provid(portrait of the everyday lives of international students and their place in the community.

> – **Emerita Professor Elspeth Jones**, *Emerita Professor,*
> *Leeds Beckett University, UK*

Vivid, complex, and rigorous, Gomes draws on her decade-long in-depth research on international students in Australia to challenge stereotypes and give international students a voice through riveting narratives and insightful analyses. Engaging and empathetic, Gomes' book is conceptually refreshing and empirically robust. A must read for policy makers, educators and practitioners in international education and beyond!

> – **Associate Professor Cora Lingling Xu,**
> *Durham University, UK*

With the notion of 'visibility', this book represents a welcome intervention in the fast-growing research on international students. Uniquely, this work foregrounds international students' place in the community, as well as their experiences told through their own voices. This engaging book is a must read for all those working on international students.

> – **Peidong Yang, Assistant Professor**, *Nanyang*
> *Technological University, Singapore*

Gomes offers a thorough and expert analysis in this book on the intricate and ubiquitous relationship between international students and the host communities in Australia. It is a must read for policy makers, researchers and practitioners in the area of international education in Australia and beyond.

> – **Jing Qi**, *Senior Lecturer,*
> *RMIT University, Australia*

International Student Visibility

This book narrates the ubiquitous relationship that international students have with their destination community, asking why students are not part of these communities despite being visible actors not only as students but as neighbours and as workers in the service industries and the gig economy.

This book examines international students living and working in Australia through a cultural and communications lens, bringing together almost a decade of interviews and online surveys. It provides insight into their transnational identities and social and cultural practices in real-world and digital spaces. Despite being an integral part of the ethnographic landscape of the places they occupy, this book argues that international students are often not an integrated part of the wider community. To remedy this, international students have found ways to explore and communicate their experiences as transient migrants in Australia. This book thus goes beyond canonical academic commentary on the international student experience – which often views them as vulnerable migrants – to suggest that students create a sense of community and belonging while providing the wider Australian public insights into the international student experience through the creative arts.

This book will appeal to scholars, upper-level students, and researchers with interests in international and comparative education, sociology of education, urban education, cultural studies, migration studies, and youth studies.

Catherine Gomes is a professor of culture and communication in the School of Media and Communication at RMIT University, Australia.

Routledge Studies in Global Student Mobility
Series Editors: *Krishna Bista and Christopher Glass*

Routledge Studies in Global Student Mobility offers a scholarly forum for original and innovative research which explores, explains, and increases understanding of issues and opportunities relating to international student mobility in K-12, higher education, and beyond. Consisting in peer-reviewed authored and edited volumes, the series advances theoretical understanding and identifies best practices for educators and professionals involved in study abroad.

As an interdisciplinary scholarly venue, the series showcases new ideas and fresh perspectives relating to international student mobility, study abroad, exchange programs, student affairs from the US and around the world, and from a wide range of academic fields, including student affairs, international education, and cultural studies.

This series is produced in collaboration with the CIES SIG Study Abroad & International Students, STAR Scholars Network, and Open Journals in Education (OJED).

Books in this series include:

International Student Support and Engagement in Higher Education
Exploring Innovative Practices in Campus, Academic and Professional
  Support Services
Edited by Janet Boyd and Mutiara Mohamad

Unintended Consequences of Internationalization in Higher Education
Comparative International Perspectives on the Impacts of Policy and Practice
Edited by Shahrzad Kamyab and Rosalind Latiner Raby

For more information about this series, please visit: https://www.routledge.com/go/routledge-studies-in-global-student-mobility

International Student Visibility
Living and Participating in Community

Catherine Gomes

R Routledge
Taylor & Francis Group

NEW YORK AND LONDON

First published 2025
by Routledge
605 Third Avenue, New York, NY 10158

and by Routledge
4 Park Square, Milton Park, Abingdon, Oxon, OX14 4RN

Routledge is an imprint of the Taylor & Francis Group, an informa business

ISBN: [9781032815855] (hbk)
ISBN: [9781032903255] (pbk)
ISBN: [9781003547082] (ebk)

DOI: [10.4324/9781003547082]

Typeset in Times New Roman
by KnowledgeWorks Global Ltd.

Contents

Preface		*viii*
Acknowledgements		*xi*
	Introducing the international student	1
1	Conceptualising the international student	19
2	International students and their place in community	36
3	'In our own words': Storifying the international student experience	47
4	Communicating with international students and why this matters	67
	Next steps	86
	Index	*89*

Preface

My first week as an international student in Western Australia was an emotional one. I remember shedding tears at the airport because I was missing my dog. The thought of not seeing her for almost a year broke my heart. I also remember wondering if this airport farewell was the last time I would see members of my family. A few days after I landed, another international student in my cohort decided to go back home because she was missing her family too much. Like me, she was a Singaporean.

That first week was also one where I had to get used to my new surroundings. While I enjoyed the coolness of the Perth climate, my living arrangements were becoming a cultural shock on a few levels. First, this was the first time I was living out of home. I had never lived anywhere else but my parents' house, which was their marital home. Second, I was living in a residential college where residents had to share common bathrooms and toilets. I am an only child and never had to share facilities with anyone other than my parents. I not only had to carry my toiletries with me but I had to get used to the lack of privacy whenever I took a shower. There were a few times when I was showering, the stall next to mine was host to people showering together. Even the toilet paper was not what I was used to.

In that first week, I made friends with other international students from Singapore and Malaysia who, like me, were missing the food we were used to. So, besides finding where the library was on campus, what was equally important was the search for the Asian foods we were familiar with. Being from Singapore, where people looked Chinese, Indian, Malay, or like myself – Eurasian – I was not used to seeing Caucasians. All of a sudden, the people around me looked like the people I used to see on television (Singapore imports a lot of Hollywood television programmes and films). While I was used to seeing Caucasians on screen, I was not used to seeing them line up with me in the dining hall of the residential college I was living in. This, together with the unappetising college food I grew to dislike and my homesickness, I wondered if I should hop on the next flight back to Singapore. As I was only 5 hours away, this really was a thought I seriously entertained. While running back home may be a thought one entertains, in reality, it is never really an option.

Being transient, international students are not like other culturally and linguistically diverse migrant communities. An obvious reason is that not only are international students transient migrants but also their presence is based on a financial arrangement with destination sites. This financial arrangement is with education providers, accommodation providers, hospitality venues, health practitioners, retailers, and tourism operators, just to name a few. International students pay for everything from their education to somewhere to live, their food, their healthcare, their consumables, and their entertainment.

The increasing expansion of international education and the economic benefits for destination countries across a range of industries means the enrolment of very large numbers of international students. In Australia, international student numbers have been climbing by the thousands yearly. Since the introduction of international student full fees in 1990, there were 2 times when international student numbers fell. The first time was in 2007–2009 as a result of negative publicity in India. This was because of 2 factors. First, there was negative publicity due to South Asian international students being left in the lurch when the 'fly-by-night', private, 'for-profit' education providers they enrolled in went bust. Second, there were news reports of South Asian international students being the targets of violent attacks, particularly in the city of Melbourne. The second time international student arrival numbers decreased was during the height of the COVID-19 pandemic, from 2020 to 2022. During this time, countries were practising strict border controls, with restrictions on the international mobility of visitors and residents.

While finishing this book, the Australian Government announced in May 2024 – through the federal budget (Australian Government, 2024a) and the draft International Education and Skills Strategic Framework (Australian Government, 2024b) released to the Department of Education – that it was going to actively reduce the number of international students coming to Australia. It said it was going to do this by capping enrolments not only at federal and university levels but at discipline programme levels too. The logic behind these caps was allegedly to reduce presumed pressures on housing availability and affordability in Australia – pressures that were blamed on the rising number of international students in the country. International students were targeted as the source of cost-of-living ills, which plagued Australia in the years after pandemic restrictions.

This book pays homage to international students not only in Australia but worldwide. My interest in international students is, in part, because I was once an international student. As a researcher, this puts me in a privileged position to present perspectives that attempt to understand and unpack the varied and rich experiences international students go through as they navigate everyday life in destination sites. These perspectives facilitate the ways in which I engage with and write about international students. As a product of international education, I believe my research has allowed me avenues to assist with international student well-being. For me, this is a way of giving back to the community I was once part of and that I continue to be a part of as an educator of undergraduate and graduate students.

References

Australian Government. (2024a). *Budget 2024–25*. https://budget.gov.au/index.htm

Australian Government. (2024b). *Australia's international education and skills strategic framework: Draft for consultation*. Australian Government Department of Education. https://www.education.gov.au/about-department/resources/international-education-and-skills-strategic-framework

Acknowledgements

This book is the result of more than a decade of work on the everyday experiences of international students in Australia. I have been blessed to have undertaken my research into the everyday lives of international students through funding from the Australian Research Council (DE130100551), IDP Education, Australian Education International, Universities Australia, Study Melbourne, Study NSW, and the National Council for Australia-China Relations (NFACR). I am thankful to RMIT for supporting my work on international students and to RMIT's School of Media of Communication – my home school – who have provided me with the time to research and write on international students.

Thank you to all the international students who have taken part in my projects and who have taken the time to tell me about their lives in Australia. It is always a privilege not only to hear stories of people's lives but also to be trusted to tell those stories.

Thank you to Krishna Bista and Chris R. Glass, valuable colleagues who have allowed me the opportunity to publish my work in this Routledge series. Both Krishna and Chris have also been supportive of my work through the years, which I am grateful for. Thank you to my Routledge editors Alice Salt and Stuti Das for facilitating the publication of this book.

Thank you to Tyson Wils for strengthening this manuscript through his expert proofreading and editing.

I have been lucky enough to have not only the friendship of Shanton Chang over the years but also his partnership in research. Shanton and I first met as first-year undergraduate international students in Australia. We then became actively involved in international student representation, which planted the seed for our research on international students. I am grateful to Shanton for the work we do on the digital engagements of international students, and for him introducing and instilling in me the sense of creating real solutions for international student well-being.

I am thankful to have a home life that allows me to write. Thank you, Andrew, for putting up with my 'just give me a few more minutes; I need to finish this sentence', and with such grace and patience. I have also been lucky to have in my life Sally, Humbug, and Scotty, who never fail to remind me when it is time for walkies, food, and cuddles – the 3 elements that are my bedrock.

I would like to acknowledge that a version of Chapter 3 '"In our own words": storifying the international student experience' will be coming out in *The Elgar Companion to Arts and Global Multiculturalism* (2025), edited by Nikos Papastergiadis, Fazal Rizvi, Sneja Gunew, and Paula Muraca. It will be titled 'Representing Themselves: International Students in the Creative Space'. I would also like to acknowledge that Chapter 4 'Communicating with international students and why this matters' builds on my previous work, *Siloed Diversity: Transnational Migration, Digital Media and Social Networks*, published by Palgrave Pivot in 2018. This book builds on work I have been doing over the past decade, which can be found in *Transient Mobility and Middle-Class Identity: Media and Migration in Australia and Singapore*, published by Palgrave Macmillan in 2017.

Introducing the international student

Introduction to this chapter

One of the earliest known international students to travel for study was a priest by the name of Emo of Friesland. Born in 1175 AD, Emo was born in Groningen in the Netherlands as a member of the Ommelanden elite, which many would consider an upper-middle-class family (OxfordVisit, 2024). Emo first studied in his home region by attending the Ommelanden Benedictine monastery, where he trained to become a priest. He then travelled to France to attend the University of Paris, where he read church law and then moved to the University of Oxford (circa 1190). He is known to be Oxford's first 'foreign student' (OxfordVisit, 2024). After completing his studies, Emo left England and returned to France again, where he enrolled in the University of Orléans. Emo had a varied career after that – first, as a teacher and schoolmaster in Northern Groningen and then as a pastor in Huizinge, which is near Groningen. At the time, Emo travelled by foot, except when he went to England, which he did by boat. As he was a trained priest reading Christianity-type courses, which were the only programmes offered during those days, he settled his accommodation issues by staying in monasteries and with clergymen. While he was not a native speaker of the languages of the education destinations he eventually settled on, he relied on 'Medieval Church Latin, Medieval English (old Frisian), and flawed French' to communicate with the locals, including the domestic students (OxfordVisit, 2024). Unlike in Emo's day, international students today can come from almost any country, they can go to almost any destination site, and they can study almost anything.

At the time of writing, global international student mobility is dominated by students coming from Asia, with China, India, and Vietnam being prominent countries. This is followed by students coming from Germany and the United States (International Organization for Migration, 2024; UNESCO, 2024). Key source countries for Australia include China, India, and Vietnam. However, Nepal, Malaysia, Indonesia, and Thailand also contribute to the number of international students coming to the country (Department of Education, 2024a, 2024b). While the English-speaking Anglosphere members – the

DOI: 10.4324/9781003547082-1

United States of America, the United Kingdom, Canada, Australia, and New Zealand – have been key traditional international destination sites, international students also travel to regional education destinations, which may also be source countries of international students. Regional refers to continental areas such as the African, European, and Asian regions. For instance, China is a key education destination for students from South Korea, Thailand, Pakistan, and India (Collier, 2023).

Back in Emo's day, students who went to study at universities in Europe were religious scholars since religion was the only discipline taught. Today, students can choose from a smorgasbord of courses across a variety of education sectors with different entry levels. International students, for instance, can enter the school system (high schools) of destination sites, undertake foundation studies leading to university entry, enrol into post-secondary institutions – specifically polytechnics and pre-university colleges – to undertake diploma courses, and be accepted into higher education institutions in order to undertake undergraduate and graduate studies. International students who enrol in post-secondary institutions can study everything from welding to cooking.

At university, students can study science, technology, engineering, and medicine (STEM) or humanities, arts, and social science (HASS) courses, if they have the entry scores to do so. Sometimes, students can combine both STEM and HASS courses as part of their degree. For instance, a student working towards a law degree may also undertake minors from STEM courses. At universities in Australia, students can enrol in associate degrees, which are pre-bachelor degrees that may run for a year, or bachelor degrees, which run for 3–4 years. Sometimes eligible undergraduate students complete an honours year following on from or as part of their bachelor's degree. At graduate level, students have the option of doing masters by coursework or masters by research degrees, as well as PhDs, doctorates, professional doctorates, and a doctor of theology. After almost a millennium since Emo's time, international students have what seems to be unending education choices.

International students, like domestic students, are able to study non-English languages at university, regardless of where they come from. However, in Australia, international students who would like to improve their spoken and written English language skills are able to enrol in English classes catered specifically for non-English speakers. These English Language Intensive Courses for Overseas Students, commonly known by the acronym ELICOS, are popular with international students who already have university degrees but who would like to improve their English language skills for professional and personal reasons. They are also popular with students who want to study diploma and degree courses.[1] In Australia, international students from non-English-speaking countries have to prove they have a working comprehension of English in order to be granted a visa to study in non-ELICOS institutions. To do this, ELICOS institutions help potential diploma and degree international students sit for and pass the compulsory International English Language Testing System (IELTS). So unlike Emo, who relied on a 'flawed' version of the local language in his destination site, international students today are compelled to improve their language skills not only for study but also to navigate their everyday encounters.

What this book does

Since the late 20th and throughout the 21st centuries, international students have been visible actors in key English-speaking Western destination sites. Australia, North America, New Zealand, and the United Kingdom have seen millions of international students go through the revolving door of transnational mobility in the quest for both a foreign education and a brighter future for themselves and their families. While international students are visible actors *in* destination communities – as students, as neighbours, and as workers in service industries (e.g. hospitality and retail) and the gig economy (e.g. delivery platform workers) – they are not *part of* these communities. By referring to almost a decade's worth of interviews and online surveys with international students in Australia about their transnational identities, and social and cultural spaces and practices both in real life and online, together with observations of international students living and working in Australian cities, this book narrates the ubiquitous relationship international students have with the destination community. This book notes that while international students are visible, they are still ignored and misunderstood. It argues that host communities need to understand them. Understanding will benefit both students and host communities. This book, however, suggests that international students have been making inroads in finding their voice with the creative space as a case in point.

The aim of this book is to unpack the relationship international students have with the destination community, where they are visible yet ignored and misunderstood; why communities need to understand them; and how students attempt to find their voice. This book acknowledges that international students have been (negatively) spoken about, written about, and researched, resulting in a cottage industry of research artefacts and media. This includes social media posts, news articles, official reports, and academic papers, seemingly dedicated to conventionalising international students as pariahs who threaten the citizenry by contributing to overcrowded cities, or as vulnerable individuals facing well-being challenges. Moreover, international students have been stereotyped in mainstream media by politicians, and in public and private conversation. International students have been vilified as permanent residency hunters and backdoor migrants, as inadequate speakers of English unprepared for higher education – thus bringing down education standards – and as groups of people who take away jobs and overcrowd housing markets. Yet, at the same time, international students are considered an economic benefit to education providers' through the full fees which they pay, and supporting secondary industries such as the tourism, hospitality, retail, housing (rental), and building sectors. Additionally, international students provide labour and services as casual workers to these very industries, as well as others such as transport, agriculture, and food processing (Chou & Gomes, 2023). Because international students are deeply embedded in the education and economic practices of destination sites, they have, in different degrees, become political targets and are also vulnerable to business exploitation and/or societal judgement and treatment (e.g. xenophobia). This is not only in Australia but everywhere they have a footprint.[2]

This book acknowledges that international students are not just transient migrants who enter a country to study, but they also have complex relationships with the places and people whose lives they are part of. International students in Australia, for instance, have been a common sight in cities, towns, and neighbourhoods that are home to universities, private colleges, post-secondary institutions, English-language schools, and sometimes high schools. Since the reopening of international borders, Australia had been seeing substantial increases in international student numbers, which were fast approaching pre-pandemic numbers of almost a million students prior to the Australian Government's decision in mid-2024 to cut new 2025 enrolments. New enrolment cuts or not, it is still challenging for international education stakeholders, such as education institutions and accommodation providers, to communicate with international students who come from culturally and linguistically diverse countries and communities. This book suggests that understanding how to communicate with international students becomes just as critical as providing them with key services framed around the duty of care. In order to comprehend the international student experience, however, it is useful to understand the appeal of travelling overseas for education.

The appeal of being an international student

Studying overseas is attractive because an overseas education is an investment in a person's future. It is *the* investment that is meant to reward a person in their professional and personal lives. The literature on international student mobility, for instance, tells us that young people, from the global south, see traveling to the global north as facilitating their economic and migrant futures (Gümüş et al., 2020; Singh, 2016; Yang & Tian, 2023). The quest for an education overseas may lead to job opportunities in the host country and thus the opportunity to migrate there permanently. Suitable work experience in the destination country may also thereafter lead to better job opportunities in the home country or elsewhere. Likewise, an overseas education in well-known institutions in the global north, particularly the anglosphere, may also enhance and diversify a person's professional credentials for easing into the employment market in the home country or even elsewhere.

Sometimes an overseas education is also attractive to the families of international students in terms of social currency. For instance, parents whose children attend well-known universities in the anglosphere have a sense of pride in their children's achievements. The literature on international student mobility also tells us that international education is a financial investment for families (Gomes, 2017; Wilson et al., 2023). International students not on scholarships are often financially supported by their families, where tuition fees and sometimes living expenses are covered by loved ones back in the home country.[3] The rewards families reap are seen in the professional and economic successes of their children, which can only be achieved through overseas (particularly higher education) qualifications.

International students in Australia I have spoken to over the past decade tell me that they think that living and studying overseas means opportunities to live and work in Australia and to obtain the skills, knowledge, qualifications, and experience to live and work anywhere in the world. In other words, the experience of living overseas is perhaps just as, or even more, important than the degree they are studying for. It is this overseas life experience that provides them with a passport for future mobility. In 2015, I wrote a paper that argued that there is a trend emerging amongst international students, where they placed global mobility to the big cities of Europe, North America, and Asia as an aspiration post-graduation (Gomes, 2015). Calling them 'footloose transients' as a play on 'footloose and fancy free', I suggested that the 60 international students I interviewed felt that their experiences as international students in Australia armed them with the tools they needed in order to pursue this exciting and romanticised life as (western) university-educated professionals. Their experiences as international students, in other words, gave them what they thought was the necessary resilience in order to live life as globe-trotting professionals.[4]

A romanticised idea about global mobility in one's personal life is broadened to include the perceived impact studying overseas has on one's personal life. An interview I did with an international student in Australia encompasses this well. Originally from Malaysia, the student let me know that she felt different to her peers who had never left Malaysia. I understood this as meaning that living overseas made her not only different but perhaps 'better' than if she had stayed in Malaysia. She explained that this was because she now had the kinds of life experiences which, if she was back in Malaysia, she would never have had. These experiences thus were shaping not only her perspectives but also herself as a person. She went on to tell me that when she gets married in the future, her husband would be like her – someone who has also had an overseas experience. While she saw herself as marrying a fellow Malaysian, she felt that the overseas experience was or would be the variable which would bind them both together. She felt that being married to someone with an overseas experience meant that he would also understand her as she would him. Her ideas about romantic relationships thus were specific in terms of the requirements for her would-be spouse. With that said, personal relationships formed during the international student experience were perceived by the students I spoke to, as the very tool necessary to survive overseas. In other words, their intentions for further mobility are encouraged by their experiences in Australia in terms of their ability to form friendship networks with fellow international students rather than with locals. Yet, at the same time, through rapid developments in communication and media technologies, they find a sense of belonging that keeps them anchored to their place of birth.

However, as the chapters in this book will describe, life as an international student is not smooth-going.

Life as an international student

During the COVID-19 pandemic, media reports and social media posts painted international students as vulnerable and in financial difficulty. This was because they could not work due to pandemic restrictions, leading to their fears of being thrown out of their rental accommodation and food precarity. What made the image of the vulnerable international student even more stark was when then Australian Prime Minister Scott Morrison (Morrison cited in Gibson & Moran, 2020; Ross, 2020) informed international students and other temporary migrants (e.g. working holidaymakers):

> As much as it's lovely to have visitors to Australia in good times, at times like this, if you are a visitor in this country, it is time … to make your way home …. At this time, Australia must focus on its citizens. Our focus and our priority are on supporting Australians and Australian residents with the economic supports that are available.

His rationale was that:

> All students who come to Australia in their first year have to give a warranty that they are able to support themselves for the first 12 months of their study. That is a requirement of their visa when they come to that first year, and so that is not an unreasonable expectation of the government that students would be able to fulfil the commitment that they gave.

Prime Minister Morrison made his statements on 3 April 2020 when Australia, like many countries around the world, made the decision to shut international borders as a way of limiting the spread of the COVID-19 virus.[5] However, for many international students, returning home was not an option. In 2020 and 2021, I interviewed international students about how they coped with the impacts of COVID-19 restrictions on their everyday lives. An international student who was completing his PhD told me that he sent his then pregnant wife back to their home country, as he felt that she would get more familial support there. He, however, would not be returning to his home country until he had completed his PhD, since he was a scientist and needed lab-access to complete his experiments. This meant missing the birth of his first-born child and the early months of their life.

For many international students, what happens in their home country may impact their everyday lives and education journeys. For instance, if the financial situation of their families is impacted, such as through job losses, bankruptcies, and other negative financial situations, international students might have to find ways to pay for fees and living costs in order to complete their degrees. Worse still, they might have to end their studies without graduating due to their inability to pay for their education and they may have to return to their home country to assist their families.[6]

While there are studies (e.g. Kristiana et al., 2022; Presbitero, 2016; Zhou et al., 2008) that note international students, like other permanent and temporary migrants, undergo culture shock, this culture shock is not so much about adapting to the national and/or ethnic cultures of the host nation. Instead, culture shock may well be more about modifying behaviours and expectations based on lack of experience as a migrant. For instance, being an international student means having to rent accommodation and, therefore, having no fixed address. Moving is a common practice with international students, where they may move every semester so as not to pay for rent if they are back in their home countries (Morris et al., 2023). In Australia, generally, undergraduate students have 2 semesters that last between 12 and 13 weeks, with the autumn semester (Semester 1) taking place from late February to the end of May, and with the winter semester (Semester 2) running from mid-July to mid/late October. The 2 main non-teaching breaks outside of these times provide the opportunities for international students to travel back home to visit their families, thus leaving their accommodation unused. To save money, particularly after the 4-month summer break, students vacate their accommodation premises permanently and store their belongings elsewhere, such as with friends. When they return to Australia, they apply for new accommodation.

For international students, living with people they don't know and sometimes in crowded conditions, are experiences they have never had. With no previous experiences living outside their immediate families and in houses or apartments outside their family homes, international students need to learn to adapt to their new living arrangements and social navigations quickly. The reality of their lack of experience living independently without their families sometimes leads to disaster. On 25 November 2014, a fire broke out in Melbourne's central business districts' (CBD) Docklands area. The fire at the Lacrosse tower, which is home to approximately 400 international students, was started by a tossed late-night cigarette left to burn in a plastic food container (ABC News, 2014). While no one was hurt in the blaze, photographs of the scene showed cluttered apartment balconies that fell victim to the fire. The fire also prompted fears that the Docklands area was becoming somewhat like an international student ghetto with residents almost exclusively living in overcrowded apartments. The fire also prompted calls for fire safety knowledge for international students (ABC News, 2015). What becomes clear is that people with little experience living on their own need to modify their behaviours to adjust to their current (transient) living situations. Yet, despite the challenges, people still desire to become international students, with Australia a key destination site.

Why Australia?

Australia is an international student country. By this, I mean that Australia is a key international education destination for people wanting to study in an English-speaking country. While international students who come to Australia do enter high schools, most often they undertake post-secondary education, particularly higher education. In Australia, 44.9% of international students pursue higher education degree programmes (Department of Education, 2024a, 2024b).[7] Moreover, Australia also consists of both state post-education providers and private 'for-profit' education providers, including higher education institutions. The private 'for-profit' providers, whose business model is based on a solely international cohort, cater to international students who are unable to enter into state institutions. International students in Australia also pay full fees for their education. Undergraduate international students pay fees that are 4 to 6 times what domestic students pay. For instance, at the University of Sydney for 2025, international students undertaking a bachelor's degree in engineering pay AUD$56,000 per year (University of Sydney 2024c), while domestic students pay AUD$10,000–AUD$11,000 per year if not on a bursary (University of Sydney, 2024b). International students pursuing a PhD in STEM pay AUD$53,500 (University of Sydney, 2024c), if not on a scholarship, while domestic students are often provided with an Australian Government Research Training Program (RTP) scholarship worth AUD$40,109 per year (University of Sydney, 2024a). So why do international students choose Australia, where fees are so high?

There are a number of reasons Australia is attractive to international students. The first reason is proximity. Australia is the closest Anglosphere

English-speaking country to Asia. The distance from Jakarta to Perth in Western Australia is just over 4 hours, while it takes only 10 hours to fly from Hong Kong to either Sydney or Melbourne and 13 hours from Mumbai to Brisbane. Hence, it is no surprise that approximately 92% of international students are from Asia – in particular Southeast Asia (e.g. Indonesia, Singapore, Malaysia, and Vietnam), Northeast Asia (e.g. China), and South Asia (e.g. India, Nepal, and Sri Lanka) (Department of Education, 2024a, 2024b).

The second reason is the quality of education in Australia. While international students come from countries with an exceptional number of higher education institutions, overseas degrees from Western English-speaking countries are often looked at favourably. In Vietnam, for instance, Australian-university-educated graduates are favoured in the job market more so than graduates from local universities.

This leads to the third reason. Sometimes, Australian higher education institutions are easier to enter than home institutions. Singapore's state universities, for instance, have high entry scores. Potential students who are unable to enter those institutions then look to Australia and other Western institutions in the English-speaking world to pursue their degrees. The National University of Singapore, for example, has a 23% acceptance rate, while the University of Sydney's acceptance rate is 70% (Edurank, 2024a, 2024b).

The fourth reason is that the degree courses are in the English language. English carries 'mobility currency' because it is considered a transnational language of communication. For instance, the British Council – a UK charity organisation that promotes 'peace and prosperity by building connections, understanding and trust between people in the UK and countries worldwide' – has over 200 offices around the world, with one of its signature activities being the teaching of English (British Council, 2024). The British Council conducts English language courses for people wanting to learn the language for everyday comprehension (i.e. General English) and for business (i.e. Business English) (British Council, 2024). Moreover, it also runs courses and conducts internationally recognised English language certification such as IELTS, which is required for visa applications in English-speaking countries. The IELTS is a necessary qualification when applying for permanent residency, and work and student visas in countries such as Australia.

Moreover, acquiring English as a foreign language has social currency. In Japan, for example, English language classes taught by expatriate staff who are native speakers (primarily Caucasians from Western English-speaking nations) are popular. This is because English language skills are seen as important by parents, professionals, and students themselves as contributing to not just employability but also key positions in the job market (Margolis, 2020). The reasons for this are simple: English is the language of international business and it is the language (or second language) of the multinational company workplace. Multinational companies, such as Fortune 500 companies Google and Microsoft, are increasingly found in Asia, Africa, and Latin America. Hence, even knowing English as a second language is a helpful skill for the local workforce.

The fifth reason Australia is a popular destination for international students is because it is perceived to be safe, friendly, and multicultural. As a case in point, marketing material by Study Australia – the department charged with recruiting future international students in The Australian Trade and Investment Commission (AUSTRADE) – sells the Australian lifestyle as much as it sells Australian education. Narratives of how safe, friendly, and multicultural Australia is, are visualised in photographs of happy young people from seemingly different ethnicities (presumably international students from Asia, Africa, and Latin America) mixing with Caucasians (presumably domestic students and lecturers) in settings that range from sharing meals together in restaurants to walking on pristine beaches at sunset.

Australia has long been imagined to be an ideal country to live in. Two international students I spoke to from Colombia said that they could not understand why Australians complained about Australia so much. They felt that Australia was safe, with excellent public transport. They then told me that in their country, violent crimes are common. In comparison, Australia was perfect for them and was the reason they chose this country as their study destination. Another international student I interviewed from India told me that she felt that Australia was the most multicultural country she knew, since here people of different nationalities, cultures, and ethnicities are part of each others' social networks.

Reason number 6 on the attractiveness of Australia as an international education destination is work rights. Before the COVID-19 pandemic, international students could legally work in Australia for 40 hours per week during semester time. During the height of the COVID-19 pandemic, international students still in Australia were seen as a viable workforce in industries desperate for workers. The agricultural industry, for instance, desperately needed workers to assist with picking vegetables and fruits, since seasonal workers who come from the Pacific Islands, and working holidaymakers (backpackers) were barred from coming into Australia due to international border restrictions upheld by the Australian federal and state governments from early 2020 to early 2022. Hence, international students were, from mid-2021 to mid-2023, allowed to work unrestricted hours during semester time. From mid-2023, however, international students were only able to work for 48 hours per fortnight. While these working hours do not seem very much compared with full-time work (approximately 72 hours per fortnight), they are still important to cover living expenses. When the COVID-19 pandemic led to mobility restrictions and curfews, international students were impacted because they worked casual jobs in hospitality and in the gig economy (e.g. personal transport), which were shut down to slow down the spread of the virus. International students reported in research (Farbenblum & Berg, 2020) and in the media (Henriques-Gomes, 2020) that the loss of casual work, as mentioned earlier in this chapter, led to accommodation and food insecurity. While families may have helped pay for tuition fees, international students still had to support themselves in their daily lives; hence, the reason gig economy jobs are popular amongst international students, specifically food delivery work (Chou & Gomes, 2023). While Australia's international education competitors, the United Kingdom and Canada, now allow international students to work 40 hours per fortnight each, Australia's biggest market competitor, the United States, does not allow international students to work unless the employment is on campus. For example, graduate students are able to work casually as teaching assistants.

The seventh reason is graduate employment. Through a special temporary work visa for Australian graduates, international students are permitted to find work. This temporary graduate work visa allows international students to stay and work in Australia for anywhere from 2 years (for bachelor degree graduates) to 4 years (for PhD graduates) (Department of Home Affairs, 2024).

This brings me to the eighth reason: the opportunity to apply for permanent residency as skilled migrants. Permanent residency in Australia is dependent on a points system based on factors such as age, work experience, education, and English proficiency. The skilled migration visa, meanwhile, favours applicants in occupations where there are skills shortages. Applicants who have undertaken their university studies in Australia score more points than those who have not studied in Australia.

Federal, state, and municipal governments, in recognising that international students are important to Australia, have established dedicated teams to promote Australia and its different states as international student destinations. Often these teams are housed in departments dedicated to developing and improving national and state economies. Understanding that reputations are built on word of mouth and, in recent years, social media posts, together with a sense of duty of care, these teams also dedicate time and energy to welcoming new international students to Australia, to the states, and to the cities even before students leave their home countries. Federal and state governments organise pre-departure information talks for incoming international students and their parents in their home countries featuring international education stakeholders. These stakeholders range from education providers to secondary industry providers who service international students, such as accommodation providers and financial institutions (i.e. Australian banks). The pre-departure talks are aimed at providing both students and parents with information about living in Australia. Such talks also function to reassure families that their children will be safe while overseas.

New international students are welcomed into Australia right after they step off the plane. State governments all around Australia set up international student 'welcome desks' that are manned by international student volunteers, who often themselves were the recipients of such meets and greets in the past. New international students are thus met by people who went through the anxieties and excitement that come with entering a new country and a new phase of life. Part of the welcome is a 'welcome pack' that provides brand new international students with information they should know for a successful time in Australia. The welcome desk is the first of many welcome experiences new international students have in the first couple of weeks of their lives in Australia. Municipal governments, which have large numbers of international students studying and living in their precincts, often have an international student welcome day. These are often organised by the city municipalities of state capitals where the CBDs are home to sizable numbers of international students. For instance, the City of Melbourne's welcome day includes a welcome address by the mayor of the City of Melbourne and orientation-week (O-week) stalls. Education providers and accommodation providers will organise a few days of orientation for new international students before the official start of the O-week festivities. While O-week includes domestic students in its festivities, the international student-specific orientation is meant to provide students with not just a welcome to Australia, to the state, to the city, to their institution, and, for many, to their new accommodation, it is also meant to provide students with information about everyday living in these destination sites.

Methodology

This book is based on qualitative research involving interviews with international students, focus groups with international students, and observations of international students and their impact on the urban cultures of Australia. The book also includes quantitative (online survey) data collected from various projects from 2011 to 2022. Contextual analysis was used to analyse the data to draw out conceptual themes. The 5 projects included in this book are: For information see Gomes et al., 2014 for Project 1, Gomes, 2017 for Project 2, Gomes et al., 2015 for Project 3, the website contactpoints. org for Project 4 and Gomes, 2022 for Project 5.

Project 1: mapping the social networks of international students: foundations for improving communication (funding agency: Australian Education International and Universities Australia)

Together with colleagues from both academia and industry focus groups were run in 2011–2012 to examine the information-seeking behaviour of international students in Melbourne. Through 7 focus groups with 36 students altogether, we explored the ways that international students accessed information regarding their health and lifestyle while in Australia. We did this by studying the relationship between international students' self-perceived identities, social roles, and social networks. We wanted to understand the patterns of communication of students. We also wanted to find out if international students in Australia were looking at Australian-based sources of information or if they relied on sources from their home countries. Our questions to the focus groups covered the participants' access to both online (e.g. websites and social media) and offline sources (e.g. newspapers and brochures). We also asked them if they consulted family and friends in the home nation, as well as friends they made in Australia with whom they communicated via digital technology (e.g. emails, social media, and other communication platforms, such as WhatsApp).

Project 2: media and transient migrants in Australia and Singapore – mapping identities and networks (funding agency: Australian Research Council)

From 2013 to 2016 I investigated the evolving cultural and social identities of transient migrants and their related social networks in a comparative study of Australia and Singapore. Transient migrants in this project included international students, exchange students, and mid- to high-level skilled workers (including those on working holidays, and professionals with degrees, working towards a degree, or about to start a degree). In other words, the project focused on a socio-economic class of mobile individuals with particularly broad skills. This focus of the study was important, as for more than 2 decades most of the work on transient migrants in Singapore has dealt almost exclusively with low-skilled labourers, such as construction workers and foreign domestic workers with few or no skills. To investigate the evolving identities of transient migrants, the project was committed to unpacking the following:

• The maintained, formed, and (re)discovered identities of transient migrants and how these identities sustain, affect, and create social networks
• The role and the impact of transient migrant media consumption and engagement in assisting and shaping these identities and networks.

This project allowed for updated research on the migration experience of the 21st century. In particular, the research developed new perspectives on integration and agency (e.g. the trend of transient migrants to become permanent residents and citizens). Moreover, the use of social media as a tool for inquiry in this highly media-centric era provided avenues for transient migrants to express their identities and create networks that permit belonging, integration, and agency – all part of the transient migrant experience.

Project 3: the relationship between social roles and information access and use of international students (funded by International Development Program (IDP) Education)

Data collection for this project took place in 2014 and was the next phase of the Project 1: mapping the social networks of international students project. It involved launching an online survey investigating the information-seeking behaviour of international students in Australia and potential international students coming to Australia. This project was particularly successful in documenting the sources that international students consulted during their stay in Australia, for example, sources relating to health, accommodation, study, news, and entertainment. These sources included personal networks (friends and family), professional contacts (e.g. education agents/recruiters), and official/public domains (e.g. institutional websites). Our online survey garnered over 7,000 responses with 6,699 of those responses from international students who were based in Australia.

Project 4: contact points: enabling international students during critical incidents (funded by Study Melbourne, Victoria State Government, and the National Foundation for Australia China Relations)

Data for this project were collected in 3 phases over a 9-month period (November 2018 to July 2019). Phase 1 focused on the key messages that emergency and health service providers wanted to convey to international students. Phase 2 focused on whether international students understood these messages and if they were willing to share the messages amongst their peers. Phase 3 focused on whether Chinese international students understood the Chinese translations of the finalised messages that could then be used in Chinese social media.

Project 5: the lived experiences of international students: pivoting on a pandemic (no funder)

Data for this project were collected from March to June 2021 via Microsoft Teams with each interview lasting around 30 minutes. There were several reasons why interviews took place online: Melbourne was in lockdown at various periods during data collection; participants were residing interstate and overseas; and the ease of conducting interviews online. For the latter, speaking to participants online meant saving time and money on travel particularly since they were not compensated for taking part in this research. Moreover, interviews, regardless of where participants were located, could be scheduled at their convenience. Eight people participated in this project.

Project 5: investigating the barriers to vaccine uptake

In this project, my colleagues and I ran 4 focus groups (2 from the Chinese-speaking community and 2 from the Arabic-speaking community) with the assistance of our community-based researchers. The community-based researchers also assisted with translation of questions and answers during the focus group interviews. Focus group interview sessions ran for 60–100 minutes. Each participant was compensated for their time with $50 e-gift vouchers from Woolworths. Each focus group was made up of 7–8 participants with 35 participants in total.

This book serves as a gateway to understanding the contemporary international student and suggests that international students are more than just learners in global higher education systems. This book argues that international students have become integral to the societies and cultures of their host nations. It points out that Western English-speaking countries have become key international education markets, which actively recruit international students leading to high numbers of foreign students circulating in host countries. With Australia as its case study, this book provides an explanation of the impact international education has had on the Australian economy, society, and culture, while introducing readers to the consequences of these impacts on the international student experience itself.

Chapter summaries

This introductory chapter has served as a gateway to understanding the contemporary international student. The chapter suggests that international students are more than just learners in global higher education systems. They have also become integral to the societies and cultures of their host nations. The chapter points out that Western English-speaking countries have become key international education markets, which actively recruit international students. This leads to high numbers of foreign students circulating in host countries. With Australia as its case study, this chapter has explained the impact this international education hub has had on Australian society and the economy, while introducing readers to the consequences of these impacts on the international student experience itself. In the following chapter, 'Conceptualising the international student', I argue that international students in Australia are visible actors in institutions of learning and visible and active participants in the broader Australian community. Next in 'International students and their place in community', I suggest that the international student is a figure who is both everywhere and nowhere. I argue that international students are not just ephemeral actors who enter a country to study but rather have complex relationships with the places they are part of and vice versa. Following this, '"In our own words": Storifying the international student experience', reflects on how creative space has become an emerging arena where international students are able to represent themselves and their experiences; while 'Communicating with international students and why this matters' observes that because international students are transient migrants, the ways in which we communicate with them should differ from the ways that we communicate with the broader resident community. Finally, 'Next steps' brings the threads of the book together with implications for policy and practice. This will be a useful frame of reference not only for Australia but for countries wishing to expand their international education sector.

Notes

1 The ELICOS Association of Australia, which is the industry association of English language or ELICOS schools, is now known as English Australia. Please see the following website for more information https://www.englishaustralia.com.au/.

2 Northeast Asian international students studying in English-speaking countries, for instance, were subjected to racism and xenophobia with the spread of the COVID-19 virus, particularly in the first year of the pandemic in 2020. This is because local populations assumed anyone who was 'Chinese looking' was to blame for causing and spreading the virus which was reported to have come out from China. At the time, there was uncertainty about what COVID-19 was other than a deadly virus which may have originated from a wet market in the Chinese city of Wuhan. At the same time, there were conspiracy theories that COVID-19 was a manufactured virus which escaped from a Chinese laboratory. Whatever its origin, Chinese and, more broadly, Northeast Asian and Southeast Asian international students and the migrant communities they come from were unfairly and erroneously blamed for being the cause of the pandemic.

3 More often than not, international students work casual jobs in order to support their living expenses – an issue this book discusses in various chapters.

4 Giving a talk about this work at a seminar in Singapore, an audience member questioned the romanticisation of this transient lifestyle. He explained that as a postdoctoral fellow, he was looking for permanence rather than transience. Originally from China, he said that he had undertaken his undergraduate studies in Singapore and completed his postgraduate work in the United Kingdom and was back in Singapore in precarious employment since he was not tenured. He explained that he had already had life as a transient professional while an international student and was now looking for an anchored life in one country. More mobility to him was not only undesirable but, he also he felt not sustainable at this time in his life. He explained that as someone in his early 30s, he felt that he needed to move onto the next phase of his life since global transient mobility is too tiring.

5 Eighteen months after Prime Minister Morrison made this statement, he encouraged international students studying remotely overseas and backpackers on working holiday maker visas to return to Australia to work in critical areas of industry such as agriculture by promising visa fee refunds (Hitch, 2022).

6 In the first year of my undergraduate degree, my worst fears were realised. My father died suddenly from a heart attack 8 months into my degree. My father's death not only impacted my well-being, especially the first few months after his death as I dealt with my own grief and that of my mother's, but also my financial situation. I was not sure how I was going to pay for my tuition fees. I ended up selling my father's car and depending on my grandmother for help to assist me with paying tuition fees while I picked up casual work here and there to pay for my living costs.

7 As mentioned earlier in this chapter, these include associate degrees, bachelor degrees, and graduate degrees. International students also come to Australia to learn English where they enrol in ELICOS (Department of Education, 2024a, 2024b) programmes for anywhere from 1 to 12 months. They may also pursue pathway programmes which include foundation courses in order to then transition into a degree programme. International students may also work towards diplomas with vocational or technical colleges.

References

ABC News. (2014, November 25). *Docklands fire: Melbourne high-rise apartment blaze forces evacuation of hundreds*. Australian Broadcasting Corporation. https://www.abc.net.au/news/2014-11-25/residents-evacuated-after-fire-in-melbourne-cbd-apartment-build/5914978

ABC News. (2015, April 28). *Overcrowding, substandard building contributed to $2m Docklands apartment fire, investigation finds*. Australian Broadcasting Corporation. https://www.abc.net.au/news/2015-04-28/overcrowding-substandard-building-contributed-docklands-fire/6426588

British Council. (2024). *About us*. British Council. British Government. Foreign, Commonwealth and Development Office. https://www.britishcouncil.org/about-us

Chou, M. H., & Gomes, C. (2023). Politics of on-demand food delivery: Policy design and the power of algorithms. *Review of Policy Research*, *40*(5), 646–664. https://doi.org/10.1111/ropr.12543

Collier, S. (2023). *8 of the best places to study abroad in Asia*. QS Top Universities. https://www.topuniversities.com/blog/8-best-places-study-abroad-asia#:~:text=8%20of%20the%20Best%20Places%20to%20Study%20Abroad,South%20Korea%20...%208%208.%20Hong%20Kong%20

Department of Education. (2024a). *International student data for the year-to-date (YTD) December 2023 - summary infographic* [Infographic]. Australian Government Department of Education. https://www.education.gov.au/international-education-data-and-research/international-student-monthly-summary-and-data-tables#toc-international-student-data-for-the-year-to-date-ytd-december-2023

Department of Education. (2024b). *International student numbers by country, by state and territory*. Australian Government Department of Education. https://www.education.gov.au/international-education-data-and-research/international-student-numbers-country-state-and-territory

Department of Home Affairs. (2024). *Temporary graduate visa - Subclass 485*. Australian Government Department of Home Affairs. https://immi.homeaffairs.gov.au/visas/getting-a-visa/visa-listing/temporary-graduate-485/

Edurank. (2024a, February 2029). *National University of Singapore [Acceptance Rate + Statistics]*. Edurank. https://edurank.org/uni/national-university-of-singapore/

Edurank. (2024b, February 29). *University of Sydney [Acceptance Rate + Statistics]*. Edurank. https://edurank.org/uni/the-university-of-sydney/

Farbenblum, B., & Berg, L. (2020, June 30). *International students and wage theft in Australia*. SSRN. http://dx.doi.org/10.2139/ssrn.3663837

Gibson, J., & Moran, A. (2020, April 3). *As coronavirus spreads, 'it's time to go home' Scott Morrison tells visitors and international students*. ABC News https://www.abc.net.au/news/2020-04-03/coronavirus-pm-tells-international-students-time-to-go-to-home/12119568

Gomes, C., Berry, M., Alzougool, B., & Chang, S. (2014). Home away from home: International students and their identity-based social networks in Australia. *Journal of International Students*, *4*(1). https://doi.org/10.32674/jis.v4i1.493

Gomes, C. (2015). Footloose transients: International students in Australia and their aspirations for transnational mobility after graduation. *Crossings: Journal of Migration & Culture*, *6*(1), 41–57. https://doi.org/10.1386/cjmc.6.1.41_1

Gomes, C., Chang, S., Jacka, L., Coulter, D., Alzougool, B., & Constantinidis, D. (2015). *Myth busting stereotypes: The connections, disconnections and benefits of international student social networks*. Proceedings of the 26th ISANA International Education Association Conference, 1–11. http://2016.isanaconference.com/wp-content/uploads/2016/02/Gomes.pdf

Gomes, C. (2017). *Transient mobility and middle class identity media and migration in Australia and Singapore*. Palgrave Macmillan.

Gomes, C. (2022). Shock temporality: *international students coping with disrupted lives and suspended futures*. *Asia Pacifc Education Review*, *23*(3), 527–538. https://doi.org/10.1007/s12564-022-09793-2

Gümüş, S., Gök, E., & Esen, M. (2020). A review of research on international student mobility: Science mapping the existing knowledge base. *Journal of Studies in International Education*, *24*(5), 495–517. https://doi.org/10.1177/1028315319893651

Henriques-Gomes, L. (2020, July 15). International students turn to foodbanks as casual work dries up in second Melbourne lockdown. *The Guardian.* https://www.theguardian.com/australia-news/2020/jul/15/international-students-turn-to-foodbanks-as-casual-work-dries-up-in-second-melbourne-lockdown

Hitch, G. (2022, January 19). *Visa fee refund offered to entice students, backpackers to fill COVID worker shortage.* ABC News. https://www.abc.net.au/news/2022-01-19/backpackers-internatonal-students-visa-fee-rebate-covid-workers/100765716

International Organization for Migration. (2024). *International students. Migration data portal.* https://www.migrationdataportal.org/themes/international-students

Kristiana, I. F., Karyanta, N. A., Simanjuntak, E., Prihatsanti, U., Ingarianti, T. M., & Shohib, M. (2022). Social support and acculturative stress of international students. *International Journal of Environmental Research and Public Health, 19*(11), 6568. https://doi.org/10.3390/ijerph19116568

Margolis, E. (2020, May 26). *Why Japan doesn't learn English.* Foreign Policy. https://foreignpolicy.com/2020/05/26/japan-doesnt-want-to-become-another-casualty-of-english/

Morris, A., Wilson, S., Mitchell, E., Ramia, G., & Hastings, C. (2023). International students struggling in the private rental sector in Australia prior to and during the pandemic. *Housing Studies, 38*(8), 1589–1610. https://doi.org/10.1080/02673037.2021.1961695

OxfordVisit. (2024). *Who was Oxford University's first foreign student? Meet Emo of Friesland.* https://www.oxfordvisit.com/articles/who-was-oxford-universitys-first-student-emo-of-friesland/#:~:text=Emo%20of%20Friesland%2C%2013th-century%20globetrotter%2C%20was%20the%20first,of%20Oxford%20%28whose%20name%20has%20survived%2C%20that%20is%29

Presbitero, A. (2016). Culture shock and reverse culture shock: The moderating role of cultural intelligence in international students' adaptation. *International Journal of Intercultural Relations, 53*(July), 28–38. https://doi.org/10.1016/j.ijintrel.2016.05.004

Ross, J. (2020, April 3). 'Time to go home', Australian PM tells foreign students. *Times Higher Education.* https://www.timeshighereducation.com/news/time-go-home-australian-pm-tells-foreign-students

Singh, S. (2016). *Money, migration, and family: India to Australia.* Palgrave Macmillan.

UNESCO. (2024). *Global Flows of tertiary-level students.* https://uis.unesco.org/en/uis-student-flow

University of Sydney. (2024a). *Australian government RTP scholarship (domestic).* https://www.sydney.edu.au/scholarships/e/australian-government-rtp-scholarship-domestic.html

University of Sydney. (2024b). *Domestic student tuition fees.* https://www.sydney.edu.au/study/fees-and-loans/domestic-student-tuition-fees.html

University of Sydney. (2024c). *International student tuition fees.* https://www.sydney.edu.au/study/fees-and-loans/international-student-tuition-fees.html

Wilson, S., Hastings, C., Morris, A., Ramia, G., & Mitchell, E. (2023). International students on the edge: The precarious impacts of financial stress. *Journal of Sociology, 59*(4), 952–974. https://doi.org/10.1177/14407833221084756

Yang, P., & Tian, Y. (2023). International student mobility in a deglobalizing and post-pandemic world: Resilience, reconfiguration, renewal. *Journal of International Students, 13*(1), i–v. https://www.ojed.org/index.php/jis/article/view/5538

Zhou, Y. F., Jindal-Snape, D., Topping, K., & Todman, J. (2008). Theoretical models of culture shock and adaptation in international students in higher education. *Studies in Higher Education, 33*(1), 63–75. https://doi.org/10.1080/03075070701794833

1 Conceptualising the international student

Introduction

When I first started researching and writing about international students just over a decade ago, there was very little work about their everyday lives. For instance, international students' social and cultural spaces in both the real and virtual worlds were not looked at as much as they are today. Instead, what researchers and the international education sector were broadly interested in were 3 distinct topics: classroom, well-being, and recruitment. Specifically, education researchers concentrated on improving curriculum planning, pedagogy, and learning; sociologists and student support staff conducted research with international students to understand and improve the international student experience; and international education recruitment agencies focused on better ways of increasing international student numbers. Additionally, because the visa status of international students is transient and temporary as opposed to permanent, international students do not have the same kinds of research urgency as forced migrants or even migrant workers. In part, this has to do with international students being perceived as 'not in trouble' and not escaping events, situations, and circumstances like asylum seekers and refugees are. Intrinsic to the notion of being an international student is the idea that a choice has been made to enter into a financial arrangement. In other words, international students are not forced to study overseas but choose to do so. This choice to study overseas is defined by their payment of fees to the institutions they are enrolled in.[1]

This chapter thus considers international students as more than just temporary migrants. Instead, they consider their overseas degree and overseas lived experiences as contributing significantly to bettering their professional and personal lives. This chapter also highlights that international students are now a growing area of academic interest. This is not only in terms of pedagogy but also studies on the lived experiences of these students. The international student experience, in other words, is not limited to the study experience – but as increasing studies are showing, the quality of life is equally important (Ramia et al., 2013). Before the COVID global pandemic, for instance, there was

DOI: 10.4324/9781003547082-2

increasing scholarship calling for a more holistic understanding of the international student experience, which is not solely steeped in the study experience but includes the lived experiences of students (Gomes, 2017, 2020; Phan et al., 2019; Tarzia et al., 2019–2022). These scholars suggest that the lived experiences of international students – including accessibility to goods and services, employment and employability, self-perceived identities, social and cultural cohesion, aspirations, and media/communication use – directly correlate with the ways students experience and perform in their degree and diploma courses.

International students in Australia

International students have had a presence worldwide for a number of decades. The International Organization for Migration (2024) notes that, in 2021, there were 6.4 million international students circulating from source to host countries in search of an education. The largest source countries are 'China (16% of all international students globally), India (8%), Vietnam (2%), Germany (2%), Uzbekistan (2%), France (2%) and the United States of America', while the preferred destinations are the United States, the United Kingdom, Australia, Germany, Canada, France, Türkiye, China, the Netherlands, and the Republic of Korea (International Organization for Migration, 2024). International students, particularly from Asia, have had a presence in the United Kingdom, Australia, Canada, and New Zealand since the commencement of the Colombo Plan in 1951. Here, soon to be former British colonies and decolonised nations sent sponsored students to be trained in skills that would assist in nation-building such as infrastructure and economic development. The late 1980s, however, witnessed Australia becoming a global player in the export of education particularly in the Asian region where Australia offered courses and qualifications that attracted students from Southeast Asia and, increasingly, from Northeast and South Asia (Adams et al., 2011). By the late 1990s and early 2000s, Australia was drawing students, particularly from South Asia who were attracted to vocational and technical programmes offered by both state and 'for-profit' education providers, whose business model almost exclusively serviced international students (Adams et al., 2011; Gomes, 2022).[2]

An integral part of Australian life

International education has changed tremendously since the Colombo Plan initiative. In 2019, a year before the COVID-19 pandemic, international students brought in close to AUD$38 billion. This figure includes fees (AUD$10 billion) and additional study and non-study-related expenses such as accommodation, entertainment, communication tools (e.g. mobile phones and Wi-Fi), hospitality, and food (Hurley, 2020; Hurley et al., 2021).[3] By the end of 2019, there were 580,000 international students enrolled in educational institutions throughout Australia (Hurley, 2020). Since the end of 2023, however, international education in Australia has been in recovery mode with 786,891 international students enrolled in Australian institutions (Department of Education, 2024). Most of these students came from a range of different countries from Asia, Latin America, the Middle East, and elsewhere. However, the majority of international students come from Asia with the top countries being China, India, Nepal, Columbia, the Philippines, Vietnam, Thailand, Brazil, and Pakistan (Australian Education International, 2024). While there are high school-going international students in Australia, their numbers are not comparable to those who are undertaking post-secondary study in universities, vocational education and training (VET) institutes, and English Language Intensive Courses for Overseas Students (ELICOS) colleges.[4]

Educating international students has thus become an education business ecology. Education providers, who are the primary beneficiaries of international education, have come to rely on the fees international students pay for their education as a form of income. This income is used for various purposes including funding research in research-intensive universities. In Australia, the Group of Eight universities are state education providers who are Australia's research powerhouses and use the income generated from international students as internal funding that is provided to research staff as well as research students. Moreover, in 2023, as part of its 'Australian Universities Accord Interim Report', the Australian federal government put forward a proposal, that universities will be taxed on the international student fees they receive (Department of Education, 2023).[5]

Meanwhile, for private, profit-making education providers, entire business models are based on the fees generated from international students. This is because the programmes offered by these providers are marketed specifically to international students. International students who enrol with these providers are attracted because they:

- Function as a pathway for students wanting to enrol into another diploma or degree programme (e.g. English language schools)
- Accept international students who are unable to enter state universities
- May be cheaper than state education providers[6]

As customers and as clients, international students also support secondary international education industries and sectors, such as the building industry, the rental market, the tourism industry, the hospitality industry, and the retail industry. Likewise, international students assist these and other industries, such as the agriculture industry and the food platform sector as service providers. International students thus can be casual workers in the following ways. As receptionists in the building and real estate industries, as tour operators in the tourism industry, as cooks, waiting staff, and cleaners in the hospitality industry, as shop assistants in the retail industry, as food pickers and abattoir workers in the agriculture industry, and as delivery couriers in the platform economy sector. International students – particularly graduate students – take up casual work as tutors and research assistants in higher education institutions, particularly universities.[7]

It is possible international students take on casual work primarily because of the cost of living in destination sites and the rising costs of international student fees. The reasons students are attracted to getting an education overseas are multifold. These include the perceived value of the diploma or degree in facilitating employability, furthering mobility and social currency. In other words, the thought of gaining internationally recognised credentials at a destination site considered to offer 'better' education standards and opportunities than what's available in the home country is intoxicating. Students believe international study will facilitate better jobs, better careers, and perhaps lead to better personal lives. However, international students who put themselves under heavy and sometimes undue pressure find that it eventually impacts their study performance.[8]

Researchers in Australia reported on the challenges international students faced as vulnerable foreigners stranded in Australia, unable to work to support themselves and facing financial precarity with cascading results, such as inability to put food on the table (Farbenblum & Berg, 2020). Moreover, Australia's education sector suffered without international students. Reports of 'for-profit' education providers and the English Australia previously known as the ELICOS sector collapsing, together with universities in deficit leading to forced and voluntary redundancies, were rife (Silva, 2021).

During the COVID-19 pandemic, the awareness that international students were necessary to the Australian economy, and to the Australian people, was seen in the increased hours students were allowed to work. In 2021, the Australian Government allowed international students to work unlimited hours during their sojourn in industries short on staff, such as agriculture and hospitality (e.g. as fruit and vegetable pickers and waiting staff, respectively). Until then, international student working hours were capped at 40 hours per fortnight during semester time. In June 2023, international student working hours became capped at 48 hours per fortnight (Department of Home Affairs, 2023). International student mobility thus is not only about international students travelling overseas to undertake study in order to create better futures for themselves but also to meet the needs of their host country. Clearly, international students are more than just temporary overseas students in Australia.

International students as transient migrants

In my work, I often refer to international students as transient migrants more so than 'temporary migrants'. This is because temporary migration and temporary migrants conjure up an ephemeral presence in a place that is not 'home', if we take 'home' to be the place of one's birth and/or the place where one's immediate family is located. Temporary migrant(ions) also invokes the idea that there is a return to the home. Transient migrant(ions), on the other hand, sees this temporality as transient before an individual moves to 'something else' and to 'somewhere else'. For international students, that 'something else' is a change of status. So, from student to graduate; from unemployed to employed; from dependent on family to independent provider for family and community; and so on. Paper qualifications, in other words, allow for transitions to be made during the course of a professional life. At the same time, that 'somewhere else' does not mean a return to the home country. Instead, it might mean going to a third country that is neither the home nor (education) host country. In other words, people who choose to study as foreigners see their status as international students as transitory and the education they receive as a stepping stone for better futures. In interviews I have conducted with international students, for instance, what comes out clearly is that they see the courses they undertake as passports to jobs in the financial cities of the world, with London, New York, and Seoul places they see themselves going to. International students thus see themselves as 'global cosmopolitans' (Gomes, 2018, p. 46). As an international student I once interviewed explained: 'the world is my oyster'.

As a result, international students see their status as both temporary and transient. It is temporary because of the finite nature of diploma and degree programmes. Diploma courses can be anywhere from a few weeks to a few months to a year or 2. Degree courses, however, take a few years. A bachelor's degree with honours is usually 4 years, while a PhD degree can also take an average of 4 years to complete. In Australia, international students undertaking PhD degrees are under pressure to complete their studies in the requisite time of 4 years due to the conditions of their visa. The visa status defines international students as temporary because they are only in the destination country for the time it takes to complete their studies. International students, however, see their status as foreigners –studying in a destination site – as transient. This is in the sense that their education qualifications will not only lead to professional opportunities, as mentioned earlier, but also bring social cache.

Paper qualifications are meant to represent skills learnt in education institutions in order to gain employment. Countries such as Australia sell international education by stating in marketing material that Australia is home to world-class education institutions where credentials from them are able to open doors to (good) positions in (good) companies anywhere in the world. For some international students, getting a degree from a foreign university – particularly if that institution is in the English-speaking West – translates to better careers when they return to their home country (Hare, 2022). Vietnamese international students, for instance, in interviews with me reveal that earning an Australian degree lifts their professional currency where they say they will be able to get management jobs if they return to Vietnam. Such jobs, they feel, are not available to their peers who entered local universities in Vietnam. At the same time, they also tell me that they do not want to return to Vietnam, just yet. Instead, they would like to work overseas, whether in Australia or elsewhere. This, they imply, provides them with the kind of overseas experience that would be even more valuable for employers once they return to Vietnam. Such aspirations, however, have of course impacted Vietnam itself, which has been reportedly undergoing brain drain (Le, 2020; Nguyen, 2014). However, the overseas study (and work) experience is interpreted by international students as providing social cache amongst their co-national peers. In talking to international students over the past decade in various projects, they indicate that they feel that they are different to their peers who had never left their home country. The world being their oyster, to them, means that they will be accumulating experiences that they would not have if they stayed 'at home'. In previous writing on transient migrants and social media (Gomes, 2018, pp. 45–46), I noted that experiences rather than tangible goods are now an indicator of standing:

> Rather than the collection of material goods which then goes on display in a person's home or? on their person (e.g. expensive jewellery), social media now allows people to collect experiences and then display those experiences by broadcasting them to friends and followers. Sometimes those broadcasts take a life of their own and become viral, reaching large circles of people. While travel-particularly to expensive, exotic or well-known locations-and mode of travel (e.g. first class in plane and train, or in private aircraft) have been signifiers of wealth and accumulated material culture, those experiences are now captured and broadcast immediately through selfies broadcast and sometimes circulated by social media and sometimes more broadly in the digital environment especially if they go viral. Social media, moreover, functions as a repository of those experiences. Not only are they easy to store or display unlike bulky souvenirs or material goods that show success (e.g. expensive vases), they are also immediately available for viewing by any social media friend, contact or follower in their own time and based on their own curiosity. For the millennial [and Zoomer) generation[s], those experiences are also indicative of the aspirations of global mobility many have accumulated ... see[ing] themselves as global cosmopolitans with ambitions to live, work, study and for a few even retire in the big cities of Europe, North America and Asia [also means] ... [n] ot having material goods to cart around might also facilitate the ability to uproot with their cultural capital intact in cyberspace.

International students see themselves as global cosmopolitans for 2 reasons. The first reason is their way of differentiating themselves from domestic students. International students in both Australia and Singapore tell me that domestic students barely speak to them and do not invite them into their friendship circles. An international student in Melbourne, for instance, explained to me that he felt disappointed that domestic students did not want to have coffee with him despite sharing common classes together. This ethnic Chinese Singaporean student interpreted this as a 'snub' based on his view that his Australian Caucasian classmates were being racist towards him. Other international students in Melbourne, who have themselves experienced unfriendly behaviour in classrooms, feel that domestic students have already developed social networks and thus do not want to invest time in friendships foreigners who one day will leave the country for good. These international students seem to cope with the unfriendliness of their domestic student classmates by giving the latter the excuse of emotional self-preservation. Here international students explain that their Australian Caucasian classmates do not want to invest in friendships with them since they are only temporarily in Australia. However, international students also provide different reasons. One way that international students deal with their (non-existent) relationship with domestic students, and perceived racism, is by claiming the 'international' in 'international student'. Here students consider themselves 'better' than domestic students due to their overseas experience in destination countries.

The second reason why international students see themselves as global cosmopolitans, particularly in the context of transience, is because they consider their experiences living, studying, and, sometimes, working casually in overseas education destinations, as providing them with the tools they need to continue living outside their home countries as workers and/or students. International students tell me that what convinces them that they can continue to live as global cosmopolitans after graduation are the life skills they learn in a foreign country without their families (e.g. domestic skills such as cooking). They also feel their ability to create social networks with other international students, many of whom become like family, also helps prepare them to be citizens of the world.

While international students are temporary migrants due to their visa conditions, which allows them temporary status in a foreign country, they are in actuality transient migrants because of their perceived continued international mobility afforded by their paper qualifications and their experiences as international students. Transient migration thus is not so much about where international students are from but rather where they are going.

International students embody transience

International students embody transience primarily because education is a transient experience. Education is a vast ecology in itself (e.g. formal school education, adult education, university education, technical education, and language education). It is also hierarchical, since individuals collect one education experience in order to embark on the next education experience. For instance, in order to receive an undergraduate education, an individual must complete a high school education and, before that, a middle school education and, before that, a primary school education. Since education is a transient experience, international students who travel abroad in order to enrol in institutions with the intention of graduating with one or more diplomas and/or degrees, already know and expect the experience to be transient. They may build their education experiences in order to achieve their end game of desired employment. For example, an international student who has aspirations to become an academic must complete a PhD degree in order to achieve the desired credentials so as to enter the academic market. However, before they are able to embark on a research degree, they must first complete an undergraduate degree and then an honours degree as the necessary pathways for eligibility into a PhD programme. Each education experience is transient because it leads to something else. Because the education experience is transient, the broader (non-study) international student experience becomes transient. International students, unlike domestic students, are anchored in Australia because this is their home country where their family homes and families are located. For international students, their family homes are still back in their home countries. Hence, where they stay in the destination country is in rental accommodation. The same international students may support themselves through casual jobs, but these jobs, again, are transient. These jobs last the duration of the education programme students are enrolled in. Upon graduation from their final education programme (e.g. a PhD), international students are no longer international students, and their status changes. They may then do one of 3 things as fresh graduates: return to their home countries, stay in the destination country, or go to a third country. These options are underpinned by their employability. In other words, graduates go where the jobs are. The COVID-19 pandemic, however, muddled this expectation of transience.

In 2021, I was interested in understanding how international students were coping with COVID-19 pandemic restrictions after a year of living either in Australia or in their home countries. What I found in the research I undertook, which was a pilot study into international students and resilience during crisis, was that my interviewees were experiencing something I termed shock temporality. Shock temporality happens when international students find that their 'professional and personal agendas and aspirations [are] in suspension due to sudden and extended temporality'. Their lives feel broken and the situation 'appears to be ongoing due to external factors outside' of their control. Furthermore:

> Individuals, thus, are unable to move on and progress in fulfilling their agendas and aspirations of which transience is the precursor. Shock temporality leads to transient migrants confronted with uncertain, precarious

and unfulfilled futures with individuals unable to move from their current point of time. Moreover, this current point of time becomes endless and may seem monotonous.

(Gomes, 2022, p. 529)

During COVID, the impact of this shock temporality left international students in a state of uncertainty and precarity as they felt their experiences and their lives were left in limbo (Gomes, 2022, p. 529). The extension of temporality disallowed interviewees from continuing their being transient in terms of transitioning to the next phases of their lives as graduates and as workers.

The international student as transient migrant thus is not only about where someone comes from but rather about where they are going. In other words, the spaces and places the transient migrant works, learns, and socialises in can be fleeting and ephemeral. By 'place', this book refers to the physical and material, such as countries and buildings, while 'space' refers to the immaterial and cultural, such as communities and groups. Some of these – in particular the education place and space – are meant to help students transition to better lives and, possibly, improved social spaces. Sometimes geographical place and space – in terms of neighbourhoods, state, and national borders – change, such as when moving because of work and career. For international students, getting an education is tied to their aspirations to experience good fortune by securing a good job that will lead to a good life. From their perspective, this can happen in their home country or in a host or third country. For international students, this education mobility can be transient itself. So, while there are international students who see further mobility (e.g. living and working in the financial capitals of the world) as their future, others see getting an overseas degree as something that will end international mobility. These students may go back to their home countries to find employment and continue with their personal (e.g. marry and start a family) and professional (e.g. rise up the ranks of a company) lives. Others decide that the country where they graduated from is the place where they will live. However, as I point out in earlier writing (Gomes, 2021), these decisions are based not only on opportunities but on events outside the control of the individual. For instance, the multinational company a person works for may have a better job for them in another country thus meaning relocation.

International students relying on each other

When I was running a focus group with international students in 2013, I asked them about what they thought about living in Australia. One of the focus group participants – a student doing a master's degree in the city of Melbourne – said that she felt Australia 'was very multicultural' because she had friends in

Australia from all over the world. These friends, however, were not Australian but fellow international students. The other international students around the table said their social circles are also made up of people from different countries. In subsequent interviews with international students that year, it was revealed that other international students do not only function as social companions but also as family who provide study and non-study support. Fast forward to 2020 and 2021 when I interviewed international students during the COVID-19 pandemic. During this period, movement restrictions were in place in Australia and participants revealed how their relationships with other international students helped them with their mental well-being. Here the participants, who were newly graduated and current graduate students, revealed how long pandemic restrictions, which to them seemed to never end, left them confined to their houses or apartments. In the city of Melbourne, for instance, movement restrictions meant that people could only leave their homes for specific reasons, such as medical appointments, caregiving, work in essential services, and grocery shopping. While exercise outside the home was allowed, this was restricted to an hour per day. International students who lived in rental housing, and whose families were overseas, felt trapped, with little to no physical interactions with anyone. This had an impact on their mental health. Participants I spoke to during those 2 years explained that the only people they socialised with, and relied on to help them get through the pandemic, were online (Gomes, 2022). In similar research conducted during the pandemic on international students and resilience, Larcombe et al. (2024) observed that international students relied on each other for emotional and practical support. International students clearly are dynamic actors deserving of academic attention.

Journal of International Students

While international students have been crossing borders in search of an education in significant numbers for a number of decades, it was only in 2011 when research interest in the international student experience took a significant turn with the launch of the *Journal of International Students* (*JIS*). Founded in the United States of America by international student from Nepal turned US academic Krishna Bista, the journal spearheaded the representation of every aspect of the international student experience, from both a US and global perspective. On its website, the journal considers the following to be the international student experience (Journal of International Students, 2024a):

- AI and technology in international education and mobility studies
- Global competence and intercultural communication
- Cross-cultural emotional wellness and psychological resilience
- Decolonization, indigenization, and the politics of belonging
- Employability, social mobility, and multinational careers

- Ethical internationalisation for greater inclusion and success
- Immigration politics, policy, support services, and human rights
- Intersectional explorations of language, culture, and identity
- New geographies of student, academic, and scientific mobility
- Science, technology, engineering, and mathematics (STEM) education, teacher education, and culturally relevant pedagogies
- Sustainability, climate change, and ecological consciousness
- Systemic reforms to advance racial justice and inclusion
- Transnational identities, networks, and communities
- Virtual mobility, virtual exchange, and online or remote learning
- Technology-enabled language immersion programmes and outcomes
- Social media and cybersecurity in international education systems

Until November 2023, *JIS* was run by a team of 4 senior editors, 4 section editors, 17 associate editors, 20 assistant editors, and a digital story and production team (Journal of International Students, 2024b). It said on its website before November 2023 that (Journal of International Students, 2024a):

> [m]ore than 300 scholars based in 45+ countries have submitted and published articles in the journal. More than half of our articles include authors from Asia, Africa, Europe, Australia, and South America … [who write about international students] … in secondary and tertiary education institutions, as well as displaced, migrant, and other immigrant student populations, including refugees, DACA holders, temporary protected status, and undocumented *minorities [and]* … international faculty, teaching assistants, and postdoctoral researchers.
>
> (Journal of International Students, 2024a)

JIS was, until November 2023, an open access journal with no processing fees. To keep the journal accessible via open access, *JIS* was a community-based project with no commercial publisher or university press behind it. Run by academic volunteers, *JIS* became a leading international education and higher education journal within 12 years since its first publication. In June 2023, the journal was ranked #9 in higher education by Google Scholar and Q1 by Scimago (Journal of International Students, 2024a).

A key theme in my writing for the past decade has been to disassociate international students from the usual theoretical and conceptual frameworks, which have provided understandings to the migrant experience. The reason for this is simply because international students are temporary migrants whose status is transient rather than permanent. While there will always be international students, and other temporary migrants, who have desires to successfully transition from temporary to permanent residency, this is not the aspiration of all international students or temporary migrants. The reasons for this include personal and professional factors as well as government policies and legislation in given jurisdictions. For instance, some temporary migrants doing low and/or unskilled work may not be eligible for permanent residency due to the conditions of their visas.[9]

Rethinking how we analyse the international student experience

Outside pedagogy and curriculum, academic studies, media commentaries, and public understandings of international students, their experiences and aspirations have often located them firmly through the lens of permanent migrant(ion) frameworks. These frameworks examine the impact of this movement which sees people and groups as moving from one destination to another with the intention of settlement, and the impact of this move on the migrants, their descendants, their communities (e.g. social conditions, social mobility), and (evolving) cultures. Some of these frameworks also examine the result of migration on place of settlement. This includes the environment (e.g. resource sustainability), economy (e.g. job creation, job insecurity), culture (e.g. impact of migrants and migrant cultures on local cultures such as food), and society (e.g. multiculturalism). The entry of migrants into a country is read across a spectrum of positives (e.g. the travelling of food cultures) to negatives (e.g. racism and xenophobia). While permanent migrant(ion) frameworks are immensely helpful in allowing for greater understandings of settler communities and their impact on destination sites (e.g. countries, states, regions, cities, and towns) through historical, contemporary, and ideological perspectives, these frameworks are not very helpful in providing analyses of temporary migrants such as international students. This is by virtue of their temporality and, therefore, transience in the destination site.[10]

While certain frameworks are helpful, such as those that point to the reception and treatment of migrants, their communities, and their descendants in destination societies, the implications towards temporary migrants, particularly international students, may differ. For instance, during the COVID-19 pandemic, there were news reports of Northeast Asian-looking (e.g. Chinese, Japanese, South Korean, Hong Kong, Singapore, and Malaysian Chinese) international students sensationally being victims of racism and xenophobia. Perpetrators of this behaviour blamed them and Asian-Australians who looked Northeast Asian, for causing and spreading the virus. Interested in finding out if international students were victims of racism and xenophobia due to the anxieties people were feeling due to COVID-19 and pandemic restrictions, I interviewed 8 international students who were current or recently graduated research students. While none of them experienced COVID-19-related racism and xenophobia, they admitted that the only times they hear of these things happening is through the media and from their families back in their home countries. An interviewee went as far as to say that he had arguments with his parents back home in China who wanted him to return after they read about racist attacks towards Chinese people in Australia on Chinese social media. He explained to me that he told his parents that after living in Australia for a number of years, he should know Australian societal attitudes better than they do.

Conclusion

While working on this book, I was also concurrently co-authoring a paper with colleagues on the reasons why international students choose certain destination sites (King et al., 2024). Here we argued that transience is a useful concept when trying to make sense of the motivations behind international student mobilities. In that paper, my colleagues and I advocated that transience can be a complementary, or even more appropriate concept, to unpack the aspirations and decision-making processes of international students when they choose where to study. However, transience as a concept is also useful in understanding international students and their experiences. This chapter has advocated that transience is a useful analytical tool not only because of the increasing numbers of students cris-crossing transnational borders but also because international students and their experiences are becoming more complex and varied. Unsurprisingly, international students have now generated greater academic interest, particularly in terms of their non-study experiences. The next chapter continues the discussion of the international student experience and acknowledges that international students have become embedded in destination communities. The chapter also observes that despite being part of the wider Australian community, not only as students but as neighbours and as service providers, international students are also misunderstood.

Notes

1 Meanwhile, migrant workers, which this book defines as temporary migrants, who travel overseas to work in unskilled or low-skilled positions, such as foreign domestic workers and labourers, do so in order to earn money for their families and sometimes villages. Migrant workers, in other words, often come from poverty and see traveling to places such as Singapore, Hong Kong, and Dubai, as the only way of earning what they consider a good income, which they remit back to their home countries. Female migrant workers thus leave their homes and families to work for families overseas as domestic workers looking after children who are not their own in order to provide for their own children in their countries of origin. Meanwhile, male migrant workers labour at the construction of buildings and infrastructure. While migrant workers feel that they are earning the kind of money they would not be able to do so in their home countries, their pay, however, is low in comparison to average salaries in host countries. For more information about migrant workers, see work by Chin (2019), Kathiravelu (2016), and Liao and Gan (2020).

2 Private 'for-profit' education providers offered diploma programmes with courses that were reflective of Australia's skill shortages. In the mid-2000s, a number of

education providers were claiming to offer hairdressing diploma courses in order to attract international students – mostly from South Asia – whose intention was not study but Australian permanent residency. Some of these education providers, however, were 'fly-by-night' companies who folded overnight. This resulted in students not only without the ability to continue their education but also out of pocket since they had to pay their semester fees upfront. The result of these business closures was, understandably, angry South Asian particularly Indian international students who, in 2006–2007, took to the streets of Melbourne to protest being treated this way (Rodan, 2008). Melbourne was the site of protests in 2009 also because of a number of news media reports of Indian international students being victims of violent street attacks or home invasions (ABC News, 2009).

3 While Australia is host to students on exchange/study abroad, this book does not include them under the banner of 'international student'. International students in this book are full-fee paying students. In other words, their education in Australia is not subsidised by the Australian Government as they way local students are subsidised. Largely international students (or their families) fund their education and living expenses in Australia through some students might be funded by scholarships from their home nations with a few funded by Australian programmes such as the as the Australia Awards which is sponsored by the Australian Department of Foreign Affairs and Trade. For more information about Australia Awards scholarships, please see the Australian Government Department of Foreign Affairs website https://www.dfat.gov.au/people-to-people/australia-awards/australia-awards-scholarships.

4 The term 'overseas student' was used more frequently in the 1980s and 1990s before the current term 'international student'. International students, today, also occupy Australian cities and towns supporting higher education institutions and high schools.

5 For an explanation of what this tax may look like, please see Ziguras and Croucher (2023).

6 International education has also evolved where reputable universities from the English-speaking West have offshore campuses, thus enabling them to directly inject themselves into source countries. Some notable universities with a transnational presence are: the University of Nottingham (United Kingdom), which has campuses in China and Malaysia; the American University, whose main campus is in Washington, DC, and has offshore campuses in Dubai and Paris; and Monash University (Australia), which has a presence in Malaysia, Indonesia, China, Italy, and India. These offshore transnational campuses allow international students to 'save' on overseas living costs while still enjoying a similar education experience. In other words, rather than travelling overseas for an (international) education, the international education comes to the student. Clearly, there are numerous opportunities to study overseas even while not going abroad.

7 When I was an undergraduate international student in the Western Australian city of Perth in the 1990s, it was uncommon for international students to take on part-time jobs in order to fund everyday living costs. International students who did take on casual work might do so on campus. Most common were tutoring and laboratory assistant work with undergraduates if the international students were graduate students or undertaking their Honours degree. Fast forward 3 decades later, it is uncommon to find international students not undertaking casual work of some sort.

8 Sometimes working casually for paid work has more contact hours than attending lectures, tutorials, and/or laboratories. A simple Google search of 'international students working in Australia on YouTube' generated pages of results. These YouTubers, who claim to themselves be international students, use their channels to inform and educate new international students about casual work. This includes employment in the gig economy as food delivery riders. A key takeaway from these videos is the number of hours they dedicate daily to working in their casual jobs meaning that they have little time to attend classes and to commit to self-directed study.

9 Temporary migrants, for instance, may be migrant workers whose visa conditions do not allow for a transition to permanent residency. In Singapore, for example, migrant workers who are low-skilled and unskilled workers, such as labourers and migrant domestic workers (maids), are on restricted visas which disallow conversion to permanent residency in any circumstance. Migrant workers are further restricted from marrying Singaporeans. While marriage in most other countries such as Australia can lead to permanent residency, migrant workers who marry Singaporeans are not provided with this option. Likewise, children of female migrant workers, who are exclusive migrant domestic workers, with Singaporeans, are not offered permanent residency. Instead, the children of such unions are required to return with their mothers to their home countries, with families split over 2 countries. Migrant domestic workers are also required to undergo medical examinations every 6 months to screen for pregnancies and for sexually transmitted diseases (STDs). If found pregnant or infected with an STD, the migrant domestic worker's visa is immediately cancelled and she will be repatriated immediately (Ministry of Manpower, 2024). Meanwhile, some temporary visas issued to skilled migrants such as knowledge workers are not based on the individual but on their employer. Individuals who work in industry for their home governments and not for profits (including religious organisations, charities, and global organisations such as the Red Cross) in paid or voluntary positions are sent by their employers to work in their organisations overseas. Here, multinational companies send their management and specialist (e.g. engineering) staff to different destination countries where they have a presence; consular staff in any destination country where there is an embassy or a high commission are most certainly working for the foreign affairs or state departments of their home countries; and employees and volunteers in not for profits go where they are needed to work for a specific amount of time. For many temporary migrants, living, working, and/or studying overseas is transient in the sense that this is an event in time for a specific purpose before returning to the home country or going elsewhere because of personal goals, aspirations, and/or situations. International students, as stated elsewhere in this book, undertake an education in order to better themselves professionally and personally. The paper qualifications they attain are used to facilitate professional mobility (e.g. getting a higher paying job as compared to having no diploma or degree qualifications) which leads to personal satisfaction (e.g. being first in family to receive a degree, the successful completion of a PhD) and social acceptability and mobility because of improved employability and employment offered by the degree/diploma.

10 Migrant(ion) frameworks are good at understanding the travelling and settlement of people from one place to another, as well as their lived experiences as individuals, communities, and descendants. However, they are less useful for understanding the impact of migration on the people and economies of the source sites (e.g. countries, states, regions, cities, towns, and villages).

References

ABC News. (2009, May 31). *Thousands protest against Indian student attacks*. Australian Broadcasting Corporation. https://www.abc.net.au/news/2009-05-31/thousands-protest-against-indian-student-attacks/1699888

Adams, T., Banks, M., & Olsen, A. (2011). International education in Australia: From aid to trade to internationalization. In R. Bhandari & P. Blumenthal (Eds.), *International students and global mobility in higher education* (pp. 107–128). Palgrave Macmillan.

Chin, C. (2019). Precarious work and its complicit network: Migrant labour in Singapore. *Journal of Contemporary Asia*, *49*(4), 528–551. https://doi.org/10.1080/0047 2336.2019.1572209

Department of Education. (2023). *Australian Universities accord interim report*. Australian Government Department of Education. https://www.education.gov.au/ australian-universities-accord/resources/accord-interim-report

Department of Education. (2024). *International student numbers by country, by state and territory*. Australian Government Department of Education. https://www.education. gov.au/international-education-data-and-research/international-student-numbers-country-state-and-territory

Department of Home Affairs. (2023). *Work restrictions for student visa holders*. Australian Government Department of Home Affairs. https://immi.homeaffairs.gov. au/visas/getting-a-visa/visa-listing/student-500/temporary-relaxation-of-working-hours-for-student-visa-holders

Farbenblum, B., & Berg, L. (2020). 'We might not be citizens but we are still people': Australia's disregard for the human rights of international students during COVID-19. *Australian Journal of Human Rights*, *26*(3), 486–506.

Gomes, C. (2017). *Transient mobility and middle class identity: Media and migration in Australia and Singapore*. Palgrave Macmillan.

Gomes, C. (2018). *Siloed diversity: Transnational migration, digital media and social networks*. Palgrave Macmillan.

Gomes, C. (2020). Outside the classroom: The language of English and its impact on international student mental wellbeing in Australia. *Journal of International Students*, *10*(4), 934–953. https://doi.org/10.32674/jis.v10i4.1277

Gomes, C. (2022). *Parallel societies of international students in Australia: Connections, disconnections, and a global pandemic*. Routledge.

Hare, J. (2022, November 22). *It's still worth it for overseas students to study in Australia, but universities could be doing more*. The Conversation. https:// theconversation.com/its-still-worth-it-for-overseas-students-to-study-in-australia-but-universities-could-be-doing-more-107180

Hurley, P. (2020). *Issues paper: International students vital to coronavirus recovery*. Mitchell Institute, Victoria University. https://www.vu.edu.au/sites/default/files/ issues-brief-international-students-covid.pdf

Hurley, P., Hoang, C., & Hildebrandt, M. (2021). *Australian investment in higher education*. Mitchell Institute, Report. Victoria University.

International Organization for Migration. (2024). *International students*. Migration Data Portal. https://www.migrationdataportal.org/themes/international-students

Journal of International Students. (2024a). *About the journal?* Journal of International Students. https://www.ojed.org/index.php/jis/about

Journal of International Students. (2024b). *Editorial team*. Journal of International Students. https://www.ojed.org/index.php/jis/about/editorialTeam

Kathiravelu, L. (2016). *Migrant Dubai: Low wage workers and the construction of a global city*. Palgrave Macmillan.

King, C., Gomes, C., Shannon, W. & Lu, R..(2024). International Student Mobility to Canada and New Zealand: "Edugration" or "Transience"?Comparative and International Education/Éducation comparée et internationale. 53(2). 46-62. https://doi.org/10.5206/ cie-eci.v53i2.17001

Larcombe, W., Ryan, T., & Baik, C. (2024). Are international students relatively resilient? Comparing international and domestic students' levels of self-compassion, mental health and wellbeing. *Higher Education Research & Development, 43*(2), 362–376. https://doi.org/10.1080/07294360.2023.2234315

Le, J. (2020, October 7). Vietnam faces increasing brain drain phenomenon. *Vietnam Times.* https://vietnamtimes.org.vn/vietnam-faces-increasing-brain-drain-phenomenon-24957.html

Liao, T. F., & Gan, R. Y. (2020). Filipino and Indonesian migrant domestic workers in Hong Kong: Their life courses in migration. *American Behavioral Scientist, 64*(6), 740–764. https://doi.org/10.1177/0002764220910229

Ministry of Manpower. (2024). *Cancel a work permit for a migrant domestic worker (MDW).* Government of Singapore Ministry of Manpower. https://www.mom.gov.sg/passes-and-permits/work-permit-for-foreign-domestic-worker/cancel-a-work-permit

Nguyen, C. H. (2014). Development and brain drain: A review of Vietnamese labour export and skilled migration. *Migration and Development, 3*(2), 181–202. https://doi.org/10.1080/21632324.2014.883243

Phan, H., Le, T., Tran, L. T., & Blackmore, J. (2019). Internationalization, student engagement, and global graduates: A comparative study of Vietnamese and Australian students' experience. *Journal of Studies in International Education, 23*(1), 171–189.

Ramia, G., Marginson, S., & Sawir, E. (2013). *Regulating international students wellbeing.* Policy Press.

Rodan, P. (2008). Dilemmas of dissent international students' protest, Melbourne 2006/2007. *Australian Universities Review, 50*(2), 33–38.

Silva, K. (2021, Marh 19). *English language colleges shut their doors as coronavirus cripples sector.* ABC News. https://www.abc.net.au/news/2021-03-19/english-language-sector-closures-borders-jobkeeper/100015146

Tarzia, L., Forbes-Mewett, H., Tran, L., Seagrave, M., Humphreys, C. F., & Murdolo, A. (2019–2022). *International student 'sexual and intimate partner violence experiences study.* Australian Research Council Discovery Project Grant.

Ziguras, C., & Croucher, G. (2023). *Occasional paper title: What are the implications of a levy on international student fees?* Melbourne Centre for the Study of Higher Education. https://doi.org/10.26188/24282697

2 International students and their place in community

Introduction

A few years ago, I was walking around a university campus in Melbourne and came across a series of life-size photographs of international students and the food they eat. Each photograph featured a smiling international student posing with their individual meals in their homes. While I found the photographs conventional and bland with students posing with the cuisines of their home countries (e.g. a Chinese student posing with a bowl of noodles), I was more fascinated with the background scenery featured in each of the photographs. Each of the photographs captured the places where the students lived. Some photographs showed clutter while other photographs featured open windows. The open windows clearly showed that international students live in high-rise buildings with views overlooking their surroundings, often office buildings in and around the central business district (CBD).

The Melbourne CBD – like all the state capital CBDs in Australia – is home or walking distance to higher education entities such as state universities and other types of education providers.[1] Hence, it is not surprising that the human subjects in some of these photographs were shown in the CBD since this area is also home to purpose-built accommodation specifically for international students. While the CBD is also the site of shopping centres, museums, art galleries, and restaurants together with office buildings, once the domestic students, shoppers, tourists, and office workers leave at the end of the day, the CBD is transformed into an international student 'demographic-scape'. International students do not only live and study in the CBD, they also often work there as waiting staff in (Asian) restaurants, as shop assistants, as cleaners of buildings and public spaces, and as food delivery couriers. International students, in other words, are all around.

The clutter, moreover, should have been the subject of the photographs because every item placed incongruously in piles tells the complex story of the life of a person living in a country alien to their own. Each photograph, in other words, maps the intersections of material culture with transience. As temporary

DOI: 10.4324/9781003547082-3

migrants, international students would have no fixed abode since they rent apartments, houses, rooms, and sometimes are subletters who rent space. For instance, while working on this book, there have been reports of international students setting up tents in living rooms as they share overcrowded apartments due to the twin reasons of a tight and an overpriced rental market (Kuang, 2023).

This chapter introduces the international student as a figure who is both everywhere and nowhere. It argues that international students are not just ephemeral actors who enter a country to study but rather have complex relationships with the places they are part of and vice versa. For instance, international students have been a common sight in cities, towns, and neighbourhoods home to universities, private colleges, post-secondary institutions, language schools, and sometimes high schools. However, despite international students being a common sight, this chapter suggests they are misunderstood by the Australian community they are part of.

International students and the city

If, you, dear reader, walk around the CBD of any Australian capital city, you will notice that you are immersed in an international student-scape. While international students may be strolling down the street with you either alone or in groups, others might be waiting outside an eatery waiting to collect food delivery orders while engrossed with the platform apps on their smartphones as they search for their next food delivery gig. You might see international students hanging out with each other at cafes and restaurants, while others might be working as cleaners quietly wiping down and disinfecting public benches. Some international students you walk past will be decked out in the latest Prada, Chanel, or another high-end fashion brand. Other international students, however, will be dressed in inexpensive track pants and sweatshirts. International students circulate in Australian capital cities because these are the places where their education providers are located. While regional centres that are located outside capital cities are home to education providers across the post-secondary spectrum, capital cities are where most public and private colleges and universities are located. Hence, a reason why 97% of Australia's international students live in capital cities and their metropolitan areas (Department of Education, Skills and Employment, 2020).[2]

The Melbourne CBD, for instance, has various educational institutions within walking distance of each other. There are 4 public university campuses: the University of Melbourne, RMIT University, the Australian Catholic University, and Victoria University, and multiple private colleges and interstate campuses (e.g. Queensland's University of the Sunshine).[3] In 2019, before the onset of the COVID-19 pandemic, Melbourne's CBD was host to 19,511 international students (Carey, 2020). This figure, which was more than double that of any other Australian suburb (Carey, 2020), was mainly due to students mostly living in purpose-built apartments catering specifically to international students. These apartments are offered by specialist international student accommodation providers such as Iglu, Journal Student Living, Urbanest, UniLodge, Atira, and The Student Housing Company. International students also find accommodation in apartment blocks integrated with office buildings and office spaces.

Accommodation in the city, whether purpose-built or provided in the form of apartments, is expensive in comparison to the private rental market further out from the city. Nonetheless, city living is popular because of the convenience of amenities. Australian cities are not only the site of education institutions but are also burgeoning with restaurants, cafes, and retail outlets. Accommodation in the city is preferable for international students who are young undergraduates living away from their families for the first time. Being vulnerable, these young people usually need structured well-being programmes, which have the dual purpose of meeting their needs and allaying the fears of their left behind families.[4] This is particularly so if they are first-year students, given that the entry level for first-year undergraduate students in Australia is 17 years of age. International students may enrol at this age or slightly older depending on what age they finish high school in their respective countries. For example, students coming from Singapore finish high school the year they turn 18 so they may enter university in Australia when they are 18 (or the year they turn 19) since Australian universities begin their first semester in late February. Parents of international students may often be willing to pay a premium price for suitable accommodation for their children, particularly if they are in their first year of university since this would most likely be the first time these students would be living, not only overseas, but away from their families.

However, living in the CBD and surrounding suburbs is expensive. This means international students, particularly those who live in non-purpose-built accommodations, such as private apartments, hostels, and landed properties (outside the CBD), end up living in overcrowded households (Knob & Cunningham, 2019). For instance, a 2-bedroom apartment in the CBD may be occupied not by just 2 people but by 4–6 people. This is so the occupants pay reduced rent through subletting. This, however, results in concern for the students who would be illegally subletting without the property owner's consent. Because Australia is expensive to live in, international students turn to casual work to pay their bills.

Work in the city

International students in Australia pay full fees for their education. This often means that they pay an average of 4 times as much as domestic students (Tran & Gomes, 2017). Though international students in Australia most often come from different levels of the middle class in their home countries, exchange rates and differences in costs of living are the impetus for students to secure part-time casual employment. The available employment opportunities are usually service industry roles that are unpopular with Australians, such as hotel cleaning and fruit picking. As a case in point, an international student I once spoke to admitted that she was working full time as a cleaner and thus found herself failing her course since she did not have the time to study. While this student was employed by a cleaning company, other international students have become active participants in the gig economy as food delivery couriers. YouTube is host to a number of international students who then advise future international students on how to become food couriers since it is the easiest employment market to enter due to having no prior experience, flexibility, and no waiting times.

However, in both of these examples, international students were also contravening their international student visas which, pre-COVID 19, stipulated that international students could not work for more than 40 hours per fortnight. If found out by the immigration authorities, they were at risk of having their student visas cancelled and thus forfeiting their education in progress. Realising that international students require assistance, not-for-profit groups such as Refuge of Hope assist students in need. Formed by former international students from Latin America now living and working in Melbourne, the group's mission is to assist with the well-being of international students from Latin America. This includes providing emergency and crisis support, including staple provisions such as rice and cereal. The group also facilitates community connections since students do not know anyone when they first come.

Despite international students from Latin America being middle class, the Australian dollar, together with the cost of living, becomes expensive ventures for them. Latin American international students are not the only ones who go through this apparent transition in class. A quarter of international students in Australia live below the poverty line (Fanning, 2016). During the first year of the COVID-19 pandemic, international students found themselves badly hit. This is because many international students were depending on hospitality and cleaning jobs to pay for their living expenses. However, pandemic restrictions saw the closure of restaurants, cafes and other eateries (e.g. food trucks), hotels, and the retail industry which employed casual workers both as serving staff and as cleaners. While international students generally took up these kinds of casual jobs, some returned to their home countries to wait out the pandemic while continuing their studies remotely online, those who stayed in Australia found themselves in financial precarity due to the lack of work available for them. This is because the only work available was for essential workers such as healthcare professionals. International students moreover were not eligible for welfare payments due to their temporary migrant status. The end of international border closures, however, has not made the living costs in Australia any better. Since 2023, for instance, international students have been returning to Australia because education is now 'business as usual' again. However, many of them have been caught out by how expensive the country has become. In particular, they highlight the high costs of the rental market with the media reporting that international students are paying higher rents and half a year's advanced rent in order to secure housing for themselves (Burgess & Wu, 2023; Lehmann & Sriram, 2020).

Of late, food delivery couriering in Australia tends to attract current and recently graduated international students. Australian post-study visa policy allows graduated international students to stay in the country for 18–48 months to work, purportedly to gain experience and to fill existing skill shortages. International students in Australia are attracted to food delivery because of the: (a) flexibility of work hours and (b) self-employment opportunities. There can also be a lack of employers in the sector. Having flexible working hours allows students to work around their studies, and not having employers means they can work almost immediately without going through the job application process. Moreover, unlike rideshare apps, food delivery apps do not require couriers to register for GST (H&R Block Tax Accountants, 2020). International students are also able to work beyond the official restriction of 48 hours per fortnight during the semester. Without GST registration, the Australian Taxation Office is unable to track the number of hours food delivery couriers work. In Australia, food delivery couriers may download as many apps as their smartphones can accommodate with many couriers freelancing across multiple apps so as to generate more bookings. During the COVID-19 pandemic, international students who had lost their jobs as waitstaff in food outlets (e.g. cafes, restaurants) turned to food delivery couriering as an income source (Riordan et al., 2021). Food delivery couriering thus is undertaken primarily for financial sustenance with no professional or future residency benefits.

Are international students misunderstood?

Despite international students having a visible presence in Australian capital cities, the 'foreign student' is still perceived within certain well-worn perceived stereotypes. First, international students are perceived to occupy either end of the socio-economic spectrum: as privileged foreigners or as vulnerable migrants. As privileged foreigners, international students are regarded as rich young people whose families pay full fees for their education and for their living expenses. This allows them to live in expensive rental apartments in CBDs. As vulnerable migrants, by contrast, international students have been considered to be living below the poverty line and thus have to take on laborious casual work in order not to face housing and/or food precarity. Both these perceptions are not completely without merit.

The perception that international students are well-to-do is perhaps rooted in the fact that they pay full fees for their education and often live in apartments in the CBD – an expensive area of real estate. For perspective, in 2024, a Bachelor of Arts at the University of Melbourne in total costs AUD $94,816–$110,824 for domestic students, while international students pay one and a half times more at AUD $146,644–$149,632 (University of Melbourne, 2024). While domestic students are able to take out a loan from the Australian Government to support their studies called Higher Education Contribution Scheme (HECS), international students do not have this luxury.[5] The image though of the well-to-do international student is more complex and nuanced than it is accurate.

The education sector in Australia is best described as an ecology. Not only are there different education programmes within both diploma and degree programmes, but these become pathways to other diploma and degree programmes that sometimes cross over. For instance, after completing a PhD degree, students may enrol in a tertiary teaching diploma – particularly important if they are working as lecturing staff. Likewise, international students come from different and varied financial backgrounds and are subject to the vagaries of foreign exchange rates. International students, for instance, may take out loans from financial institutions in their own countries in order to cover their education fees while working casual jobs to support themselves. I spoke to an international student enrolled in a private college in Melbourne who told me that she was working full-time as a cleaner in order to support herself. While it is not unreasonable to assume that international students may come from middle-class families in their home countries, the foreign exchange rate coupled with costs of living makes studying overseas an expensive venture. On Mercer's index for cost of living in 2022, Melbourne is ranked Number 67, while Hanoi is ranked Number 150 (Mercer, 2023). In dollar terms, the cost of living in Hanoi for a month is AUD$990, while the cost of living in Melbourne is AUD$3,276. Living in Melbourne for Vietnamese international students, by way of example, is more than 3 times the cost of living in Hanoi (LivingCost, 2023). Meanwhile, the average salary in Australia is AUD$69,888 (Jobted, 2023), while the average salary in Vietnam is AUD$28,246.34 (Average Salary Survey, 2023). Australians, in other words, earn almost two and a half times more than Vietnamese people. This discrepancy in earning power across both countries means that families have to save enough money in order to send their children overseas for a university education.

Meanwhile, the perception of international students as vulnerable captured public attention during the start of the COVID-19 pandemic and the accompanying movement restrictions. In Australia, international students reported widespread housing, food, and financial precarity (Farbenblum & Berg, 2020) because of the closure of non-essential businesses, which employed international students as casual staff. International students were also excluded from support accorded to the rest of the resident population. This is even though international students are taxpayers.[6] Emergency responses from state governments, state universities, and non-government organisations, such as Foodbank, while well-founded, were insufficient to support international students during the pandemic (Lehmann & Sriram, 2020). Meanwhile, outbreaks of xenophobia seen international students blamed for causing and spreading

COVID-19, while social isolation and indefinite separation from family due to travel bans have exacerbated stress and alienation (Gomes et al., 2021). Returning students barred from re-entry, meanwhile, experienced different stresses as lives were placed on hold due to uncertain or halted study futures and career aspirations. The pandemic, in other words, exposed experiences students never experienced, our lack of understanding of students in crisis, and how to help them. In 2023, with the erasure of all COVID-19 travel restrictions leading to the opening of all international borders, Australia welcomed international students back into the country. While education providers celebrated the return of international students, the students found themselves encountering the unexpected challenges of finding suitable housing. International students landed in a country in the midst of a housing crisis. The influx of international students at the start of 2023 exacerbated the already saturated housing market leading to students having to pay upfront and in advance above the rental market price, and/or share with other international students in already overcrowded premises. Some education providers also resorted to encouraging their staff to provide emergency housing to students. Unsurprisingly, international students faced accusations of causing the Australian housing crisis (Lehmann, 2023) in the public domain.

This brings me to my second point. International students are stereotyped into one, more, or all of the following categories: as permanent residents; as foreign students taking away university places for domestic students; as foreigners who take away casual work (e.g. waiting on tables) from Australians and as graduates who take away office jobs away from Australians; as migrants whose presence raises the costs of living and thus make affordable housing rentals difficult for Australians; as contributors to overcrowding in capital cities especially the CBDs; and as weak learners who are unable to communicate in English in an acceptable (Australian) standard thus contributing to the dumbing down of subjects. These stereotypes have dominated public and private discourses with international students being a hot button issue especially during elections. For instance, in the 2019 Australian general elections, then Prime Minister, hopeful, Bill Shorten accused international students of taking away jobs from Australians (Sukkar, 2019).[7]

In 2015, I co-wrote an opinion piece where we pointed out that such stereotypes are harmful to international students (Tran & Gomes, 2015). Here we pointed out that stereotyping international students widens the gulf between international and domestic students where generalising international students makes them not only feel disconnected but also puts them in a position of marginalisation in the classroom and on campus. Moreover, stereotyping international students has destructive impacts on their access to work placements and employment in Australia due to employers having preconceived notions about international students and international student graduates. The issue with stereotyping is that it positions international students as 'a problem' to be dealt with, rather than focusing on the benefits international students bring as useful constructors of knowledge (Tran & Gomes, 2015).

My third and final point has to do with the perception that international students kept to themselves throughout their time in Australia. International students, of whom many come from countries that are culturally and linguistically diverse to Australia, may find difficulties finding Australian friends. International students tell me that they feel that Australians, particularly domestic students, do not want to socialise with them for a variety of reasons. Some believe Australian students are racist while others believe that they themselves are the problem. For instance, there are international students who reason that their lack of proficiency in the English language contributes to difficulties in forming social connections. As a result, they put in effort to improve their language skills. Other international students feel that because they are only in Australia for a short time, domestic students do not want to invest time into friendships with them. Surprisingly, some international students tell me that they feel little commonality with Australians who are ethically similar to them. Asian international students I spoke to, for instance, felt that Asian-Australians (e.g. Indian-Australians, Chinese-Australians, Vietnamese-Australians) were 'more Australian' as one interviewee from India told me. He said that while Indian-Australians may look like him, they are not like him and were out of touch with India. He explained:

> I found that people of Indian origin who have been outside India for one generation or so, have lost their touch with India to such an extent that, for me seeing from this perspective, there's not much of a difference between a person who is not a native Indian at all and a person who is settled out of India except for one generation or so. Even, for example, people settle in Australia for more than one generation, they can speak my language, understand me, facial expressions are similar and all, but for me they're as good as local Australians.

Meanwhile other Asian international students outrightly state that Asian-Australians – those who were born in Australia or grew up in this country – prefer to socialise more with 'white' Australians than with them.[8] Hence, Greek-Australians, Italian-Australians, and Australians from Latin America may be understood by international students as 'white' due to visual markers such as pale skin, light-coloured hair, and light-coloured eyes. In Asian countries such as Singapore, these markers are recognised broadly and understood as 'white' because the local entertainment media portrays people with these characteristics as white. *The Noose* (Anand, 2007–2016), a popular made-in-Singapore skit show that ran from 2007 to 2016, for instance, featured a character called Barbarella played by actress Michelle Chong, who was enamoured with Eduardo Saverin who she referred to as her 'ang moh' boyfriend. 'Ang Moh' translates to 'red hair' in Hokkien and is used as a descriptor in Singapore and Malaysia, and to a lesser extent Taiwan and Thailand, to refer to white people. Billionaire Saverin, who is one of the co-founders of Facebook, however, comes from a Brazilian-Jewish family.

Conclusion

Walk down any street of an Australian state capital CBD and the chances of bumping into international students are extremely high. Students from Asia, Africa, Latin America, Europe, North America, and the Pacific may be strolling down the streets, buying groceries, enjoying meals at eateries, hanging out with each other, and working as servers, cooks, cleaners, and delivery couriers. Despite being visible members of the larger Australian community, international students, however, are often misunderstood. Such misunderstandings are often based on preconceived notions of international students within the very community the students live in, circulate, and serve. While such preconceived notions are hurtful in the worst of times, since they are rooted in stereotypes, they may also impact on the ways in which international students and others in the Australian community communicate with each other. Chapter 4, for instance, looks at why communication with international students is critical, particularly concerning their well-being which impacts their experience as international students and therefore as transient migrants.

Notes

1 Private education providers are 'for-profit' companies that provide foundation, diploma, and degree courses. Their business models are based on full-fee-paying international students as their core student body. English language education providers are those who teach English and whose international student body comes from non-English-speaking countries.
2 As of 1 June 2022, the Australian Government's Department of Education, Skills and Employment has been split into 2 entities: the Department of Education and the Department of Employment and Workplace Relations.
3 The private colleges and interstate campuses enroll students for both degrees (undergraduate and graduate) and diplomas (e.g. English language).
4 To provide context, a one-bedroom apartment in purpose-built international student accommodation in Melbourne which is located in the CBD is estimated to cost between AUD$329 and $699 a week in 2023. This price also includes air-conditioning, utility bills, Wi-Fi, 24-7 security, furniture, and an events programme. However, a shared rental house or apartment in inner city Melbourne is estimated to cost around AUD$275. This estimate excludes utilities, Wi-Fi, or cleaning, which purpose-built accommodation provide. Hence, a student living in purpose-built accommodation might be spending between AUD$17,108 and $36,348 a year for rent and board, while a student living in private rental away from the CBD though in the inner city will be spending AUD$14,300. The difference in money spent for rent and board in other words can be AUD$2,808–$22,048. See estimates in Rivett (2023).
5 For more information on HECS, please see the following website: https://www.studyassist.gov.au/help-loans/hecs-help.

6 The federal government of Australia responded to the crisis by developing 2 tax-payer-funded financial schemes – JobKeeper and JobSeeker – to assist Australians and Australian permanent residents. According to the Australian Tax Office Website, 'The JobKeeper Payment scheme is a temporary subsidy for businesses significantly affected by coronavirus (COVID-19). Eligible employers, sole traders, and other entities can apply to receive $1,500 per eligible employee per fortnight' (see Australian Taxation Office, 2024). Meanwhile JobSeeker, according to Services Australia (2024), which is 'responsible for the delivery of advice and high-quality, accessible social, health and child support services and payments', provided 'Financial help if you're between 22 and Age Pension age and looking for work. It's also for when you're sick or injured and can't do your usual work or study for a short time'.

7 In a lecture I gave to undergraduates on the experiences of international students and working holidaymakers in Australia, a student in the class asked me: 'Don't you think all these temporary migrants take away jobs from us Australians?'. What took me by surprise was the context of the subject I was lecturing in. This was a Migration Studies subject which the student was enrolled in as an elective. Such subjects take a non-confrontational perspective of migrants in the sense that they often frame migrants as vulnerable (e.g. victims of racism and xenophobia) and seeking humanitarian assistance (e.g. refugees and asylum seekers). These courses also look at the economic benefits migrant bring to destination sites in terms of filling in labour shortages as mobile subjects seek professional opportunities to better their lives.

8 International students consider 'whiteness' as inclusive of not only Caucasians but anyone who did not neatly look Northeast Asian, South Asian, or to a lesser degree, Southeast Asian.

References

Anand, P. (Writer). (2007–2016). *The noose* [TV series]. Channel 5; Mediacorp.

Australian Taxation Office. (2024). *Tax file number*. Australian Government Australian Taxation Office. https://www.ato.gov.au/Individuals/Tax-file-number/

Average Salary Survey. (2023). *Vietnam/salary*. https://www.averagesalarysurvey.com/vietnam

Burgess, A., & Wu, K. (2023, May 19). *International students faced with housing and cost-of-living stress say they were misled about Australia*. ABC News. https://www.abc.net.au/news/2023-05-19/international-students-migrant-housing-crisis-living-costs/102355508

Carey, A. (2020, June 14). The Melbourne suburbs the international student drought will hit hardest. *Sydney Morning Herald*. https://www.smh.com.au/education/the-melbourne-suburbs-the-international-student-drought-will-hit-hardest-20200614-p552el.html

Department of Education, Skills and Employment. (2020). *International students studying in regional areas*. Australian Government Department of Education. https://internationaleducation.gov.au/research/Research-Snapshots/Documents/Location%20of%20International%20Students%20in%202019.pdf

Fanning, E. (Host). (2016, March 30). *Many of Australia's international students are living well below the poverty line* [Audio Podcast]. Australian Broadcasting Corporation. https://www.abc.net.au/listen/programs/lifematters/7283500

Farbenblum, B., & Berg, L. (2020, June 30). *International students and wage theft in Australia*. SSRN. http://dx.doi.org/10.2139/ssrn.3663837

Gomes, C., Hendry, N. A., De Souza, R., Hjorth, L., Richardson, I., Harris, D., & Coombs, G. (2021). Higher degree students (HDR) during COVID-19: Disrupted routines, uncertain futures, and active strategies of resilience and belonging. *Journal Of International Students*, *11*(2), 19–37. https://doi.org/10.32674/jis.v11iS2.3552

H&R Block Tax Accountants. (2020, April 8). *Tax deductions for Uber Eats and other delivery drivers*. https://www.hrblock.com.au/tax-academy/tax-deductions-delivery-riders

Jobted. (2023). *Average salary and wage in Australia*. https://au.jobted.com/salary

Kuang, W. (2023, April 4). *International students resorting to pitching tents in living rooms as rental shortage bites*. ABC News. https://www.abc.net.au/news/2023-04-04/international-students-resort-to-living-in-tents/102179212

Lehmann, A. (2023, March 1). *'Are you asking us to sleep under the Harbour Bridge?': 3 myths about international students and the housing crisis*. The Conversation. https://theconversation.com/are-you-asking-us-to-sleep-under-the-harbour-bridge-3-myths-about-international-students-and-the-housing-crisis-200274

Lehmann, A., & Sriram, A. (2020, August 31). *4 out of 5 international students are still in Australia – how we treat them will have consequences*. The Conversation. https://theconversation.com/4-out-of-5-international-students-are-still-in-australia-how-we-treat-them-will-have-consequences-145099

LivingCost. (2023). *Melbourne, Australia: Cost of living, prices for rent & food*. https://livingcost.org/cost/australia/melbourne

Mercer. (2023). *Cost of living*. https://www.mercer.com/insights/total-rewards/talent-mobility-insights/cost-of-living/#rankings

Riordan, T., Robinson, R., & Hoffstaedter, G. (2021). "I don't have money to pay rent" but "I feel free": How migrant food delivery workers use agency to overcome precarity in the "Gig" economy. In *CAUTHE 2021 Conference Online: Transformations in Uncertain Times: Future Perfect in Tourism, Hospitality and Events: Proceedings of the 31st Annual Conference*. CAUTHE. https://search.informit.org/doi/10.3316/informit.700562471992256

Rivett, D. (2023, August 24). *Cost of living guide for students in Melbourne*. Scape Student. https://www.scape.com.au/scape-stories/finance/cost-of-living-guide-melbourne-students/#:~:text=The%20average%20cost%20of%20living%20in%20Melbourne%20for,you%20factor%20in%20items%20such%20as%20health%20insurance

Services Australia. (2024). *Newly arrived resident's waiting period, Services Australia*. Australian Government https://www.servicesaustralia.gov.au/individuals/topics/newly-arrived-residents-waiting-period/30726#:~:text=New%20residents%20may%20have%20to,use%20most%20of%20our%20services

Sukkar, M. (2019, July 16). Work rights visa out of control, Bill Shorten says. *The Australian*. https://www.theaustralian.com.au/nation/immigration/migration-program-flexible-michael-sukkar-says/news-story/5498966ab70064120f41c30db50e5f3c

Tran, L., & Gomes, C. (2015, April 30). *Stereotyping international students is unjust*. University World News. https://www.universityworldnews.com/post.php?story=20150428141315340

Tran, L., & Gomes, C. (2017). Student mobility, connectedness and identity. In L. Tran & C. Gomes (Eds.), *International student connectedness and identity: Transnational and trans-disciplinary perspectives* (pp. 1–11). Springer.

University of Melbourne. (2024). *Tuition fees and other study fees*. https://study.unimelb.edu.au/how-to-apply/fees

3 'In our own words'

Storifying the international student experience

Introduction

International students have been spoken, written, and researched about resulting in a cottage industry of social media posts, news articles, official reports, and academic papers dedicated to conventionalising international students as pariahs, economic booms, and vulnerable individuals. International students have been stereotyped in mainstream media, by politicians, and in public and private conversation as permanent residency hunters and backdoor migrants, as inadequate speakers of English unprepared for higher education thus bringing down education standards, and as groups of people who take away jobs and overcrowd housing markets (Tran & Gomes, 2015). Yet, at the same time, international students are considered an economic benefit who not only fuel education providers' coffers through the full fees which they pay but also support secondary industries such as the tourism, hospitality, retail, and building sectors but also the rental market. Moreover, international students provide labour and services as casual workers to these very industries as well as others such as transport, agriculture, and food processing. Because international students are deeply embedded in the education and economic practices of destination sites, they have not only become political targets but also vulnerable to business exploitation and societal judgement and treatment (e.g. xenophobia). However, how have international students voiced their own experiences with people and cultures in destination sites?

By weaving in my experiences as an international student and as a scholar writing about multiculturalism and creative works this chapter looks specifically at two diverse creative mediums where international students in Australia have found a space for (self) representation: the television situation comedy and the theatre. In particular, I look at the American-based and Malaysian-born former Australian international student Ronny Chieng's television series *Ronny Chieng: International Student*, and the international student theatre event *Act of Translation* whose cast is made up of international

DOI: 10.4324/9781003547082-4

student performers narrating and relating on their experiences in Australia. This chapter thus discusses the rich experiences of international students who use the creative realm to have entertaining, funny, and poignantly honest conversations with audiences about their (multicultural) experiences with Australians, with Australian culture, and with each other. This chapter also acknowledges that while the international student voice is now making inroads into the creative space, it does so through conventional stereotypes as a way to engage with audiences. However, before I discuss how international students use their own voice to discuss and express their experiences as foreigners studying in Australia, I briefly point to how international students are often thought of in this country.

Conventionalising international students in public discourse: a schizophrenic concept

Traditional media and social media conceptualise the international student in schizophrenic terms as both villain and victim depending on perspective and political angle. On the one hand, international students are stereotyped negatively as villainous threats to Australians. Here international students are conventionalised in the following ways:

- Not serious students but backdoor migrants using international education as a pathway for permanent residency.
- Bringing down academic standards.
- Unable to speak English well or if at all.
- People who take away university places from Australians.
- Contributing to the unemployment of Australians by taking away jobs from them.
- Are a hotbed for Chinese Communist Party activities due to the presence of Chinese international students.
- Are the reason for overcrowding in the central business districts (CBDs) of Australian capital cities since most universities and private post-secondary and higher education providers are located in the CBD.
- Are the cause of the housing crisis in Australia since international students prevent Australians from access to affordable rental accommodation.

On the other hand, international students are also considered to be people who are victims because they:

- Are cash cows for universities since the full fees they pay are used for internal funding for research institutions.

- Are suffering from mental stress due to a myriad of reasons such as loneliness, homesickness, and financial difficulties.
- Face homelessness due to a lack of suitable accommodation where they are the end result rather than the cause of the Australian housing crisis.
- Are having difficulty putting food on the table due to financial difficulties.
- Have to resort to laborious and long hours in the gig economy as transport and delivery workers due to the lack of available casual employment.

Scholarship, however, in Australia and elsewhere tends to analyse the international student experience from a well-being lens as evidenced by the work of Forbes-Mewett (2019), Marginson (2014), Sawir et al. (2008), and others. While there have been pioneering inroads by international education scholars to create a space for international students to discuss their experiences first-hand and provide them with a form of agency (e.g. the open access *Journal of International Students* edited by Krishna Bista and Chris Glass), there are very few examples of international student narratives in the creative space. Cinematic productions featuring international students as protagonist are few and far between with the 1984 Hollywood film *Oxford Blues* starring Rob Lowe as an American international student in the United Kingdom perhaps the only one in existence. Former international students have, however, written memoirs about their experiences as young people coping with life overseas. Recent examples include Rajika Bhandari's *America Calling: A Foreign Student in a Country of Possibility* released in 2021 about the author's reflections not only on her life as an international student but what international education means for her personally and culturally; and Sukant Suki Singh's *Limitless Humans: How Running Helped Me Live a Meaningful Life* published in 2020, on how running marathons helped with his mental health while an international student in Australia. Both these books were passion projects and published independently by the authors themselves.

What the limited number of creative fiction and non-fiction projects on international students in the creative space shows us is that despite the fact that international students have a strong presence in popular destinations such as North America, Australia, the United Kingdom, and New Zealand, international students may not be considered 'interesting' to wider audiences. Narratives about international students, whether fictional or biographical, are niche. This is because international students are transient and perceived to have little impact as individuals or as a complex group in the popular imaginations of the countries they study in. Moreover, international students do not get the same amount of attention or evoke the same kind of romanticised Bildungsroman or sympathetic characteristics of other transnational migrant figures, such as refugees and asylum seekers. Or perhaps cinema and the book are not the best creative platforms to tell the story of the international student.

Before discussing international students and the creative artefacts featured in this chapter, I would like to first highlight how creative work can be a canvas for reflecting on society.

The creative canvas and multiculturalism

When I first started working on this chapter, ChatGPT was causing much contestation in the news media and on social media platforms. Educators, artists, and technology commentators were debating the benefits and pitfalls of this new technology. At my university, as with other education institutions, teaching staff were at their wits end about how to stop students from using ChatGPT for their assignments. However, some research staff saw this new technology as simply a tool which enhanced the ways in which they could better communicate the results of their research (e.g. using ChatGPT to conduct literature review searches). For me though, when ChatGPT came out, the first thing I thought of was 'Skynet', the evil technological entity which caused the destruction of humanity and dominated a dystopian Earth of the future in the *Terminator* film franchise (Cameron & Hurd, 1984–present). So, what do ChatGPT and the *Terminator* film franchise have to do with multiculturalism and the creative space?

I have been a long-time fan of science fiction in film and television. Academic colleagues in cinema, television, and cultural studies, together with cine-buffs and fans, recognise that science fiction presents us with a glimpse into the future. Gene Roddenberry's 1960s *Star Trek* series (1987–1994), for example, introduced us to mobile phone and tablet technologies decades before these became ubiquitous with everyday life in the 21st century. *Star Trek*'s series sequel *Star Trek: The Next Generation (TNG)*, together with the *Terminator* franchise, presented us with descriptions of artificial intelligence (AI) which were both helpful and deadly. In *TNG*, for instance, the android Lieutenant Commander Data and Captain Jean-Luc Picard helmed Enterprise's on-board computer were both not only helpful but funny and personable. Data's evil android brother Lore together with Skynet and all the Terminators sent to kill resistance leader John Conner and his mother, however, were the villains of the piece. Whether portrayed as essential tools or as harbingers of a dystopian future, the creators, writers, cast, and crew of these modern classic tales were more than masterful storytellers. They were able to convey, visualise, discuss, debate, critique, and generate ways of thinking of the challenges societies face from creative if not honest perspectives. The creative space, in other words, is, in many ways, an acceptable avenue to think, display, and discuss societal issues and challenges of the present while contemplating a society of the future. While science fiction does this well as the acceptable space for creative futuristic truth-telling, this genre is not the only avenue for such contemplations. The creative space's ability to not only capture large international audiences' imagination but the impact that comes from being a site for discussion about contemporary social issues is arguably second to none. The same can also be said about academic commentaries on multiculturalism in cinema.

Since the late 1990s, scholars have recognised the creative space's ability to discuss and explore multiculturalism. This is not only in migrant destinations but also in settler societies whose histories were built on colonial legacies. In Australia, Tseen Khoo (2003), Jacqueline Lo et al. (2008), Dean Chan (2005), and others have been recognising the significance of the creative space in spearheading Asian-Australian representation so much so that they formed a collective of academics and creatives known as the Asian Australian Studies Research Network (AASRN) in 1999. In Southeast Asia, Gaik Choo Khoo (2009, 2011) acknowledges the importance of Malay cinema in unpacking the complexities of religion and gender in multi-ethnic yet Malay-dominated Malaysia, while K.P. Tan (2009) critiques ethnic stereotyping in Singapore cinema and television. For Tan, stereotypes are not only damaging for ethnic minorities but serve to convince the broader Singapore population that clichéd generalisations represent multicultural harmony. Tan's overview of ethnic stereotyping in the Singapore film and television landscape notes that while audiences identify with these stereotypes in order to enjoy the productions, they do so as a way of coping with their anxieties about their ethnic 'Other'. These anxieties are supported, if not instigated, by Singapore's scripted history, which highlights that threats to Singapore's stability come in the form of ethnic minority dissatisfaction (Gomes, 2010; Hong & Huang, 2008). Tan writes:

> [I locate] within popular film and television the ethnic stereotypes that implicitly inform multiracial policies and which are in turn reproduced by the coupling of commercial demands with the monomaniacal and rigid pursuit of national security. In other words, stereotypes on film and television are supplied to audiences who demand an immediately gratifying means of helping them deal with the perceived ethnic threats, more recently foregrounded by popular historical accounts of ethnic hostilities in Singapore. These accounts have come to constitute a large part of the official material for "National Education" in schools and the wider public.
>
> (Tan, 2009, p. 289)

Almost a decade ago I released my first book – *Multiculturalism Through the Lens: A Guide to Ethnic and Migrant Anxieties* (Gomes, 2015).[1] This book used Singapore cinema as a voice which echoed the ways in which Singaporeans viewed ethnicity, migrants, and the government's approach to migration. The chapters I wrote collectively argued that Singapore cinema

represented the 'heartbeat of the nation'. I argued that Singapore cinema stori-
fied and visualised the insecurities Singaporeans felt about their place in Singapore through their anxieties about ethnicity and migrants. *Multiculturalism
Through the Lens* was a passion project which weaved different scholarly
and personal threads together. My doctoral training was firmly rooted in film,
cultural, Chinese, and historical studies with my PhD specifically examin-
ing women warriors of Chinese language cinema. My thesis looked at the
impact and significance of strong women not only to thrill audiences but also
as symbols of Asian feminism and Asian modernity. While my research since
then has become ethnographic and empirical, I have always held a soft spot
for creative work. Creative works' ability to not only capture large international audiences' imagination but the impact that comes from being a site for
discussion about contemporary social issues is significant. *Multiculturalism
Through the Lens* was an opportunity to discuss ethnic minorities in Singapore from the perspective of being an ethnic minority myself. I was born and
bred in Singapore as a Eurasian – an ethnic category which makes up 0.6% of
the population (Pereira, 2015). Singapore's multicultural policy, however, is
grounded within a Chinese-Malay-Indian-Others (CMIO) racial[2] framework
with ethnic categories governing everyday life. To illustrate, any official and
non-official document (e.g. raffle tickets) requires identifying one's ethnic
category. The CMIO categories, while reflective of the major ethnic groups in
Singapore, relegate Eurasians within the 'Others' category. Hence, throughout
my life growing up in Singapore, I always ticked the 'Others' box.

While this chapter champions the creative space as an exciting and honest avenue to discuss multicultural matters, it would be remiss of me not
to point out that this space also sometimes presents a commentary which
can be very wrong and extremely dangerous. *Multiculturalism Through the
Lens,* by way of example, discussed the portrayal of Eurasians in Singapore
cinema. Here I wrote about how the Singapore films I looked at portray
Eurasian characters as visually loud caricatures such as bumbling clowns
or effeminate man-boys. Often these characters were foils to the central
ethnic Chinese hero. While these local films (e.g. *Army Daze*, 1996; *One
Leg Kicking,* 2001) were popular amongst Singaporeans, they also cast an
exceptionally long stereotypical shadow on an entire minority group in Singapore. The task of writing about Eurasians was to call out the perpetuation
of minority stereotypes for laughs.

Meanwhile for generations, Hollywood, the world's most successful and
impactful entertainment industry with a distribution network second to none,
has had a long history of creating stereotypes of non-Caucasian culturally and
linguistically diverse (CALD) communities. Northeast Asians, for instance,
have historically been portrayed throughout the 20th century as villains bent
on world domination (e.g. Fu Manchu), evil Dragon Ladies exacting cruelty
as henchwomen (e.g. any character played by legendary Asian-American actress Anna May Wong), and buck-toothed imbeciles (e.g. Mickey Rooney's

Mr Yunioshi in 1961's *Breakfast at Tiffany's* directed by Blake Edwards). While the 21st century has seen greater diversity in Hollywood with *Crazy Rich Asians* (Chu, 2018) being lauded rightly or wrongly as a beacon for (Northeast) Asian representation and the 2023 Oscars respectively giving Malaysian-born ethnic Chinse Michelle Yeoh and former Vietnamese refugee Ke Huy Quan the best actress and the best supporting actor awards, there have been occasions when these inroads still seemed impossible. Yellowface – where white actors play Northeast or Southeast Asian characters – such as when Scarlett Johansson played the title in the live action feature of popular Japanese anime film *Ghost in the Shell* (Sanders, 2017), still happens. Meanwhile Muslims – particularly Middle Easterners – are portrayed as religious fanatics and terrorists, particularly after the suicide terrorist attacks of 9/11 in 2001. Hollywood and the broader 'Western English-language cinema', which includes the United Kingdom, Australia, and New Zealand, are not the only cinemas which function on stereotypes to drive plots, sub-plots, character development of major and minor characters across genres such as dramas (action, political, and crime), thrillers, police procedurals, and comedies amongst others.

To illustrate, one of the most successful television shows in Singapore – *Under One Roof* (Teo et al., 1995–2003) – once featured Australian/British backpackers who were portrayed as unwashed, freeloading, hippish dumpster divers. Meanwhile, Hong Kong cinema of the 1980s and 1990s almost exclusively portrayed Caucasian men as either villains or bureaucratic buffoons as depicted in any Jackie Chan film (e.g. *Police Story* in 1985 and its sequels released in 1988, 1992, 1993, 1996, 2004, and 2013; Chan et al. 1985–2013). Both Singapore and Hong Kong were colonies of the British Empire, and these portrayals may be ways in which both these visual mediums dealt with their colonial histories. Singapore has often attributed its economic success as an act of decolonial necessity while its citizens have taken pride in the country's ability not only to punch above its weight on the world stage but also to maintain conservative values as the backbone of Singapore's moral code. These elements provided Singaporeans with a keen sense of nationalism which was the glue that bound this multicultural nation state. Meanwhile, Hong Kong cinema's portrayal of British men specifically in government positions, such as administrators and police chiefs, in productions prior to the 1997 handover of Hong Kong to Chinese from British hands, represented the sense of betrayal Hong Kong people felt with being passed from one colonial power to another. During the golden age of Hong Kong cinema (1984–1997), Hong Kong people and their cinema had an interconnected and interdependent relationship with one another (Teo, 1997). Here Hong Kong cinema had the ability to feel and then visualise the pulse of the Hong Kong people, while Hong Kong audiences could recognise and identify with what they saw on screen (Teo, 1997). The golden age of Hong Kong cinema started the year when then British Prime Minister Margaret Thatcher and then Chinese paramount leader

Deng Xiaoping signed the agreement for the transfer of Hong Kong from British to Chinese hands.

Ethnic and gender stereotypes have been used to frame and discuss a range of issues. These include social, economic, ethnic, ideological, religious, communal, community, and political issues and anxieties. Skin colour, for instance, is a visual marker which immediately invokes assumed knowledge based on the audience's collective understandings of race, gender, and class regardless of accuracy (Marchetti, 1994). Scholars and cinephiles have long discussed the harms such representations have done on CALD migrant communities. However, what happens when minorities take charge of their own representation? From 1998 to 2001 the British Broadcasting Corporation (BBC) aired a comedy sketch television show called *Goodness Gracious Me* (Bhaskar et al., 1998–2001). Based on a BBC Radio show a few years earlier, *Goodness Gracious Me* featured an entirely British South Asian cast of characters played by British South Asian actors, written by British South Asians, and created by British South Asians. *Goodness Gracious Me* then paved the way for a related British comedy talk show *The Kumars at No. 42* (Sardana, 2001–2006) which was the brainchild of the creators, writers, and actors from *Goodness Gracious Me*. While both shows featured South Asian stereotypes as the collective backbone of their comedy, these were used as commentaries on South Asian integration, diasporic community practices, and British entertainment media's portrayal of South Asians (which involved the cast parodying Brownface portrayals of South Asian characters). It is expected, and understandable, that creative practitioners from the CALD citizenry groups would make use of the creative space to highlight the multicultural community's social and cultural experiences in the adopted country. This is because the adopted country is home to members of multicultural communities who are themselves migrants or descendants of migrants. However, what happens when transient migrant CALD creative practitioners adopt the creative canvas to discuss their multicultural experiences in the host country?

International students

I first started researching the everyday experiences of international students in the early 2010s. I was still an early career researcher trying to find research areas which I was passionate about and which excited me. The prospect of researching the social, cultural, and digital spaces international students occupied fascinated me particularly since, at that time, not much was written or spoken about how international students went about their everyday lives outside of study. I was not trained as an ethnographer but I wholeheartedly embraced the idea of talking to people to understand their stories. A decade later, my research on international students has expanded to include understanding student well-being and providing practical solutions to help students navigate their online and offline surroundings while overseas.

My interest in international students stems from the fact that I too was an international student – both as an undergraduate and as a postgraduate – in Australia. I was an international student in Perth in the state of Western Australia before returning to Singapore – the place of my birth – to work. Six years later, I returned to Australia. This time, it was to Melbourne in the state of Victoria to enrol in a PhD programme. I had no scholarship both times. While I was blessed that my parents paid for my undergraduate tuition and living expenses, I was, however, on my financial own while undertaking my PhD. So, I worked 3 jobs at any one time to put food on the table and a roof over my head. I sorted out my tuition fees by cobbling money I saved from working in Singapore, using an inheritance left to me by my grandmother and by borrowing from a friend. I went against one of the prevailing stereotypes at the time that international students were well-to-do.

While writing this chapter, the stereotype of international students as 'rich kids' has somewhat been tempered with industry and news reports showing that international students face hardships. This includes financial insecurities leading to food and housing challenges made visible, particularly during COVID-19 lockdowns and restrictions (Farbenblum & Berg, 2020; Gomes et al., 2021; Qi & Ma, 2021). To me, researching about international students has been a natural progression in terms of highlighting not only the day-to-day challenges they face but also their agency. This is because I was also a student activist while an undergraduate in Perth. As an activist, I often highlighted international student issues as the first female international student to be Treasurer of the Guild of Undergraduates.

Researching international students, however, is not only a passion project; it is a necessity, particularly in Australia. I live and work in Melbourne which is currently home to 182,000 international students hailing from approximately 120 countries (Australian Trade and Investment Commission, 2023). While 2020–2022 saw huge reductions in international student numbers due to the COVID-19 pandemic, 2023 saw the international education sector recover. This recovery was due to 3 factors:

- International borders being fully opened
- The Australian Government halting online learning for university coursework programmes (Australian Skills Quality Authority, 2022)
- The decision by the Chinese Government not to recognise overseas degrees attained by Chinese citizens while in destination countries

In other words, international education is now business as usual with Melbourne living up to its reputation as an international student city.

Significance of international students

In 2020, there were 6.3 million international students (International Organization for Migration, 2023) worldwide. This was up by 2 million from 2000 (International Organization for Migration, 2023). Migration scholars also tell us that international students are likely to become permanent residents or workers in the countries where they study. Moreover, countries such as Singapore, Australia, New Zealand, the United States, and Canada recognise international students as potential members of the workforce. In Singapore, for example, international students, while unable to work during their studies, are provided with incentives to work in local companies as knowledge workers after graduation. Singapore offers international students bonded scholarships where upon graduation from a local university, students then work in Singapore companies for a period of 3 years directly after graduation to meet labour demands.[3] Meanwhile, other countries such as Australia see international students as filling in an employment void. Australia allows international students to work 48 hours per fortnight to fill vacancies in areas and industries desperate for workers. Often these job opportunities may not reflect the courses international students are enrolled in, but rather involve labour-intensive, if not back-breaking work, in hospitality and agriculture. Here international students perform services such as cleaning (hospitality), fruit/vegetable picking (agriculture), and abattoir work (agriculture) (Gomes, 2022). When international students and backpackers were restricted from coming into Australia during the COVID-19 pandemic, media outlets were writing and sharing distressing reports on food waste as produce was left to rot due to the inability to find fruit and vegetable pickers while farmers faced debt (Bolton, 2023; Green, 2023; Russo & Barnsley, 2022). Meanwhile, the price of chicken meat rose due to the lack of abattoir workers. People in Australia found that their food and grocery bills rose. This not only impacted vulnerable Australians but transient migrants also found it difficult to put food on the table.

The presence of international students in destination cities and countries also changes the culture and feel of the environments they occupy. In Melbourne, where I live, the central business district (CBD) reflects the vibrancy international students bring to the area. Besides being host to high-rise purpose-built accommodations for international students, Melbourne's food and retail scenes cater to the needs of international students, particularly those from Asia. Chinese, Korean, Malaysian, and Indian eateries dominate while shopfronts with Chinese signages and Korean fashion boutiques are common sights. In addition, a cottage industry servicing solely international students involving commercial, government, not-for-profit (e.g. advocacy), well-being, and academic industries has firmly developed to help students before, during, and after their time in destination sites – most of which have little to do directly with study. Clearly, international students have a significant impact on the places, cultures, economies, and societies they become intrinsically tied up with during (and after) their sojourn as students. With all this said, it is surprising that the international student has not been used as a key character or narrative device to drive creative plot and storylines. That is, not until now. This chapter looks at 2 creative works featuring the international student as the driver of the narrative and as the performer. The first is television situational comedy (sitcom) *Ronnie Chieng: International Student* (Chieng & Fay, 2017), while the second is a theatrical event called *Act of Translation* which is both the title of the play and the theatre company. Both are based on the experiences of real international students. However, while former international student Chieng uses these experiences to fuel a fictional series, which he has creative control over, *Act of Translation* is fuelled by the real-life experiences of its international student performers. While *Ronnie Chieng: International Student* relies on comedic devices, such as stereotyping, to get laughs and highlight subtle themes (e.g. cultural differences), *Act of Translation* (Simmonds, 2017) uses the real stories of international students narrated by the student-performer themselves who directly talk to audiences about the challenges they face. Both, however, highlight the international student experience as a multicultural experience. This is because both show how international students navigate cross-cultural relationships and situations while living overseas.

Ronnie Chieng: International Student

In 2017, comedian Ronnie Chieng's limited sitcom series *Ronnie Chieng: International Student* aired in Australia. This 7-episode series was a fictional account of Chieng's experience as an international student studying law at the University of Melbourne.[4] *Ronnie Chieng: International Student* was not only co-created and co-written by Chieng but also starred Chieng as himself. When *Ronnie Chieng: International Student* first came out, I thought the series would mirror my own experiences as an international student since I am an alumnus of the University of Melbourne. It was thrilling to see various parts of the university featured in a television programme about international students who, like me, also lived in one of the university colleges. I was enamoured by how accurately the series portrayed the relationships international students have with each other, the 'international student' lens each episode used to view the foreignness of Australian university student culture, and the quirkiness of Asian international students themselves. While these were done through some familiar stereotypes (e.g. the hard-drinking white Australian student and the Asian food-obsessed Asian international student), they were also done with an acerbic commentary which only a 'fictional' comedy could realise. Let me explain.

All the main student characters in this sitcom were not Melbournians (Melbourne residents). The international student characters were Asian and came from Malaysia, China, and Vietnam, while the exchange student came from the United States. Asher, the only Australian student, hailed from a farming family in regional Victoria. *Ronnie Chieng: International Student* really is telling the story of how young people adapt to and navigate around the challenges associated with being a fish out of water. Ronnie's friendship circle is completely made up of quirky international students and Asher. In my own research on the non-study experiences of international students, a key finding is the significance of friendship circles in the entire international student experience. International students who I interviewed in not only Australia but also Singapore tell me that their only friends are other international students (Gomes, 2015, 2017, 2022). The primary reason they tell me is because only other international students understand the international student experience (Gomes, 2015, 2017, 2022). These tight-knit friendship circles create not only community and belonging (Tran & Gomes, 2017) but also provide students with the well-being and support they need (Gomes, 2015, 2017, 2018, 2022; Gomes et al., 2015, 2021). During the COVID-19 pandemic, for instance, international students revealed that they turned to other international students for help for almost everything to do with well-being.

Ronnie Chieng: International Student, however, is also littered with stereotypes about Australian culture and Asian quirky traits. Here Australian drink culture and left-wing university political performance are highlighted with comedic effect. In the first 2 episodes of the series, Australians are portrayed as scruffy, ill-mannered drunks who spend time either drunk in a pub or drunk in the backyard of a conventional notion of an Australian university student's house – a dilapidated workman's cottage terrace decorated with Nepalese prayer flags. In another episode, the act of a student protest drives the narrative. Here the episode starts with Ronnie helping Asher out by manning the student-led organic food co-op shop. Audiences see the co-op through Ronnie's disgusted eyes where he comments that the 'open yogurt has animal hair' and that the shop 'is a hygiene situation, [and that the proprietor] 'should throw this shit out'. The same proprietor and his 'hippy' friends then protest a bubble tea shop – the only Asian eatery on campus – claiming it to be a form of globalisation. The bubble tea place, however, as explained by Chinese international student Wei-Jun (played by Chinese-Australian actress Shuang Hu), represented a sense of home to the Asian international students in the series. While this episode stereotypes the Australian university student as overtly political, it also does critique protest culture. This episode single-handedly critiques Australian student politics as in itself being cluelessly racist while protest culture as being no more than performatory.

Being a comedy, the series unashamedly uses stereotypes to drive plot and storylines. However, these stereotypes provide the audience with layered and complex narratives that highlight the international student experience in Australia. A recurring character in the series is Ronnie's mother. The audience only sees Mrs Chieng on Ronnie's phone whenever she calls him from Malaysia to FaceTime him. While, on one level, she comes across as the stereotypical nagging mother warning him not to pick up bad Australian habits like drinking and 'getting girls pregnant', on another level, their conversations reveal the dual spaces of identity international students need to balance. Here Ronnie attempts to be the 'good Malaysian son' by studying hard which, he reminds his mother, he does whenever she calls to check up on him – often while he is in a lecture theatre. At the same time, he is also attempting to distance himself from this identity by embracing the experiences accorded to him as a young man living overseas as an undergraduate student. Here he is not only encountering first-time experiences such as unrequited love but also experiences which would get him into trouble in Malaysia, such as drug use. In the latter, Ronnie tries methamphetamines to help him keep awake while he studies for his exams. The hilarity, of course, is that he takes more than he should and is highly energetic and unpredictable throughout the episode. In Malaysia, methamphetamine trafficking carries the death penalty, while its use may lead to incarceration (CountryReports, 2024).

While stereotypes are often used to drive comedies not only for laughs but also as satire, there is the danger such devices become offensive. By way of example, popular United Kingdom and Hollywood sitcoms during their day such as *Are You Being Served?* (Lloyd & Croft, 1972–1985), *Seinfeld* (David & Seinfeld, 1989–1998), *Little Britain* (Walliams & Lucas, 2003–2006), *Two and a Half Men* (Lorre & Aronsohn, 2003–2015), and *Home Improvement* (Finestra et al., 1991–1999) have, by today's standards, become critiqued, to various degrees, for their transphobia, fat-shaming, disability shaming, and racism. *Little Britain*, for example, was pulled out from the online streaming platforms BritBox, Netflix, and BBC iPlayer almost 2 decades from when it was first aired (BBC News, 2020). While I do not think *Ronnie Chieng: International Student*'s use of stereotypes as a comedic device is offensive today, in 20 years' time, new audiences might differ in their opinion due to changing societal norms. The same doubts cannot be had though for *Act of Translation*.

Act of translation

In the same year as *Ronnie Chieng: International Student* was released, Melbourne-based theatre director Catherine Simmonds worked with international students to create *Act of Translation*. Funded by the City of Melbourne, *Act of Translation* became a phenomenon with international student well-being stakeholders. This was not only in Melbourne but also more widely in regional Victoria where there are regional university campuses and education providers. Featuring international students studying and living in Melbourne, *Act of Translation* featured these students not only as actors but also as storytellers of their own experiences in Australia.[5]

The student-performers – mostly studying English language courses or enrolled as undergraduates or postgraduates in state institutions or with private providers – highlighted issues they faced connected to their own mental well-being. These included coming out as LGBTIQ+, dealing with cultural differences, accommodation issues, and experiences with part-time employment. For instance, the international student performers discussed the language barriers they faced where English, the only official spoken and written language in Australia, contributed to their mental stress because English was not their first language. Another member of the cast gave a poignant description of how she did not want to disappoint her mother because she is lesbian. For many people in the room, the experience of this student-performer was alien. The student, who is originally from China, relayed how being lesbian is disappointing to her parents since she is an only child and thus expected by both her parents and Chinese society to marry and have children. Australia, she explained, provided her with the freedom to come out and deal with her sexual identity. The cast discussed how they had to quickly come to terms with Australian cultural traits. As one student-performer explained: 'I don't understand why Australians always say fuck this, fuck that, fuck everywhere'. The cast revealed how they never imagined how expensive living in Australia would be and, therefore, had to live in shared accommodation arrangements which had more people than legally allowed. They explained how they must resort to lying to landlords in order not to be evicted from their overcrowded dwellings. To cope with the living expenses, they also take on laborious jobs as cleaners and waitresses; jobs they admit they would never do in their home countries.

Act of Translation was no doubt a powerful theatrical event which not only highlighted the challenges international students in Australia encounter through vignettes. The play also provided the student-performers with agency since they used their own voice to narrate their individual experiences. However, an issue I was confronted with watching the play and the accompanying documentary was the collective nature of the international students themselves.[6] While the play featured an entire cast of international students, I could not actually name any individual – unlike the cast of characters in *Ronny Chieng International Student*. In part, this was because the cast of *Act of Translation* was much bigger than the cast in Ronnie Chieng's sitcom. However, international students are not a monolithic community but individuals with different personalities, dynamic identities, and varied aspirations. In 2018, I authored a book called *Siloed Diversity: Transnational Migration, Digital Media and Social Networks* which pointed out that the international student community represents diversity. The book is based on a variety of research projects and data from thousands of international students I had surveyed and interviewed in the preceding 7 years in Australia and Singapore. I argue that international students have diverse backgrounds coming from different national, language, cultural, ethnic, and socio-economic groups. Even coming from the same country does not mean cultural and language singularity as in the case of not only Singapore but also Malaysia, which is multicultural, multi-ethnic, multilingual, and multi-faith. Moreover, international students not only have differing everyday face-to-face experiences in the destination neighbourhoods, towns, cities, and countries they study in but also differing digital experiences despite growing up with the internet. For example, the way Singaporeans write on social media platforms, such as Facebook, Instagram, Snapchat, WhatsApp, and so on, will be different from the ways in which other nationalities write on this platform. Singaporeans may use Singlish (Singapore English) – which is a quite common way of speaking English – in their posts on social media. Non-Singaporeans would not understand this language unless they spent considerable time living in Singapore (Chang & Gomes, 2017).

Ronnie Chieng: International Student appealed to a broader audience since it is a televised comedy which has had a continuous second life on paid channels Comedy Central, Netflix, Apple TV, Google Play, the Australian Broadcasting Corporation iView website, and also on pirated websites. *Act of Translation*s does not have such a reach, despite being freely available as an online documentary on the City of Melbourne's YouTube channel. For instance, the first episode of Chieng's series has, at the time of writing in May 2023, 692.2K views on Comedy Central's YouTube channel while the *Act of Translation* documentary only has 5.7K views.

The reach of *Act of Translation*'s narrative, themes, and messages was further restricted primarily because, the show was a theatrical event. I suspect too that the play may have been, as the saying goes, preaching to the choir. When I attended the *Act of Translation* performance as well as aligned performances (e.g. Be You Be Seen as well as productions by Story Is Connection), the audience was almost exclusively made up of supporters who work with international students and more widely in the international education sector. It also consisted of international students themselves.

While *Act of Translation* may have performed to audiences already familiar with the international student experience, the play still provided the added benefit of cultural context leading to (multi)cultural understandings. These understandings however were not limited to audiences. In the *Act of Translation* documentary, the international student performers relate how the play not only allowed them to vocalise their multicultural experiences with Australians and Australian culture but also with each other. This is because the cast was made up of international students from different nationalities, who, through their own admission, would not have otherwise met. The play, to them, facilitated the opportunity not only to meet but also to create bonds with international students from other nationalities, cultures, and ethnicities. Friendship circles, which were mentioned elsewhere in this book, in other words, transcend familiar markers of identity established before studying overseas. As a result, new relationships can be created through the shared unique experience of being transient international students.

Conclusion

Discussions of multiculturalism are often centred on the citizenry while omitting transient migrants who temporarily live in a country. However, transient migrants such as international students, though temporary, affect the multicultural mosaic of the countries in which they study. This can be seen not only in changes in the ethnographic landscape but also the food and cityscapes of the places in which they live. For instance, in Australia, food cultures have evolved and come to reflect the cuisines of the countries students come from. At the same time, the look and feel of the CBDs host to education providers (e.g. universities and private colleges) have undergone physical changes with purpose-built housing for students and the circulation of international students becoming significant features (Gomes, 2022). While international students have been the subject of political, economic, policy, academic, and media discourses concerning international education, migration, population control, and finance, where international students are spoken about, this chapter reflected on how the creative space has now become an emerging area where international students are able to represent themselves and their experiences. *Ronnie Chieng: International Student* and *Act of Translation*, though quite different productions, are trailblazers primarily because they put the international student at the centre of the narrative. Both provide a voice for international students while relating the international student experience as a series of varied multicultural experiences with the host nation and with each other.

While there are clearly positives in terms of international student self-representation, the characters in both the fictional *Ronnie Cheng: International Student* and the real-life international student performers in *Act of Translation* presented characterisations which themselves are steeped in conventional stereotypes. Could this be because the creative space is an environment where conventional stereotypes are a necessity for audience engagement particularly when the subject matter is about 'the Other'? Here I go back to K.P. Tan's (2009) astute observations of Singapore film and television earlier in this chapter, where he points out that in order for audiences to truly understand 'the Other', representations of 'the Other' need to be built on conventional stereotypes. Conventional stereotypes, according to Tan, not only make palatable the characters on screen but also what they represent in reality. Stereotyping international students, even in productions where the international student voice is both dominant and arguably authentic, still becomes a necessity not only for audience engagement but also for audience acceptance of the concept and figure of the international student.

Moreover, for international students who are the creators, writers, and performers, relying on stereotypes to engage with their audiences is unsurprising. International students are transient migrants in the study destinations which are their temporary rather than permanent homes. The impact of their portrayal of those stereotypes may not be felt on both personal and conceptual levels. Ronnie Cheng, for instance, may have spent a decade living in Australia as an international student and then as a comedian, but at the time of writing, is neither a citizen nor permanent resident of this country. Based in New York as a senior correspondent for *The Daily Show* and a rising star in Hollywood while still a citizen of Malaysia, the chances of Cheng coming back to Australia to live and work are slim. While Australia may have educated him and launched the early part of his career, Cheng's emotional ties and future do not lie in this country. In other words, as transient migrants, international students are not anchored to the study destination. While some may stay as permanent residents or even as citizens, they no longer live or identify as international students. Therefore, the stereotypes they relied on to push narratives about themselves, and their experiences, no longer impact them. Nonetheless, these stereotypes do live on as artefacts in the creative space and community at large.

Notes

1 In the book I suggested that while on the surface Singapore seemed like a successful multicultural nation where people from diverse ethnic backgrounds live harmoniously together, the country is instead a place where citizens struggle with anxieties over ethnicity, which in Singapore is known as race. I further suggested that these anxieties were compounded by the increasing numbers of new migrants (skilled workers who can become permanent residents and unskilled temporary guest workers) entering the country. The foundation of Singapore's multicultural identity is made up of three broad ethnic groups – Chinese, Malay, and Indian (CMI) – with the Singapore-born Chinese by far being the largest community at almost 80% of the population. While there is an 'Others' category which allowed Singaporeans such as Arabs, Armenians, and Eurasians to be classified. However, these ethnic groups are not as culturally nor ethnically recognizable because of their relatively small numbers. I further suggested that communities or individuals outside of these recognizable classifications are viewed with trepidation by Singapore society. Hence, the new (permanent and transient) migrants entering the nation state – many of whom come from the ancestral homes of locally-born Singaporeans and from the surrounding Southeast Asian region – created such unease and angst amongst citizens leading to unabashed displays of xenophobia in public online spaces. In other writing, I also note that these xenophobic feelings are actively displayed in the private spaces amongst family and friends (Gomes, 2015).

2 In Singapore, ethnicities are referred to as races. So Chinese, Malay, Indian, and Eurasian ethnicities are known as races. However, for the purpose of this paper, I use the term 'ethnicity' and its derivatives rather than 'race'. This is because while race often broadly refers to physical markers such as facial bone structure ethnicity often refers to markers of culture and tradition.

3 The Singapore Government provides bonded scholarships to bright international students. It is worth noting that entry into a local institution is highly competitive and based solely on merit.

4 While a second season was planned after the success of Season 1, Chieng's career thereafter took off. He relocated to New York City after getting a job as a correspondent for the *Today Show* with Trevor Noah, and for regular acting roles in Hollywood television series (e.g. as Dr Lee in *Doogie Kameāloha, M.D.*; Kang, 2021–present) and in film (e.g. as Edison 'Eddie' Cheng in *Crazy Rich Asians*; Chu, 2018).

5 *Act of Translation* led to a complementary play with the same concept called Be You Be Scene (Stories at the Heart of Change) the following year and a theatre company called Story Is Connection which was active at the time of writing – all based in Melbourne.

6 See https://www.youtube.com/watch?v=xhVSzGzUAjE.

References

Australian Skills Quality Authority. (2022, October 19). *Education services for overseas students - ESOS National Code: Return to compliance.* https://www.asqa.gov.au/news-events/news/education-services-overseas-students-esos-national-code-return-compliance

Australian Trade and Investment Commission. (2023). *Victoria. Capital City – Melbourne.* Study Australia. Australian Government Australian Trade and Investment Commission. https://www.studyaustralia.gov.au/en/life-in-australia/locations-in-australia/victoria-melbourne

BBC News. (2020, June 9). *Little Britain pulled from iPlayer and Netflix because 'times have changed.'* British Broadcasting Corporation. https://www.bbc.com/news/entertainment-arts-52983319

Bhaskar, S., Syal, M., & Gupta, A. (Creators). (1998–2001). *Goodness gracious me* [TV series]. BBC.

Bolton, M. (2023, May 2). *At an average of $6 each, soaring pineapple prices are here to stay.* ABC News. https://www.abc.net.au/news/2023-05-02/high-pineapple-prices-set-to-stay-/102292266

Cameron, J., & Hurd, G. A. (1984–present). *Terminator* [Film franchise]. Paramount.

Chan, D. (2005). Playing with race: The ethics of racialized representations in e-Games. *International Review of Information Ethics, 4*, 24–30.

Chan, J., Tong, S., Chan, B., & Ding, S. (Directors). (1985–2013). *Police story* [Film franchise]. Golden Harvest.

Chang, S., & Gomes, C. (2017). International student identity and the digital environment. In I. Steglitz & B. Kappler (Eds.), *Learning across cultures: Locally and globally* (pp. 39–62). NAFSA: Association of International Educators.

Chiang, M. (Screenwriter). (1996). *Army daze.* Cathay Asia Films.

Chieng, R., & Fay, D. (Creators). (2017). *Ronny Chieng: International student* [TV series]. ABC Television.

Chu, J. M. (Director). (2018). *Crazy rich Asians.* Warner Bros. Pictures.

CountryReports. (2024). *Criminal penalties in Malaysia.* https://www.countryreports.org/country/Malaysia/criminal-penalties.htm

David, L., & Seinfeld, J. (Creators). (1989–1998). *Seinfeld* [TV series]. NBC.

Edwards, B. (Director). (1961). *Breakfast at Tiffany's.* Paramount Pictures.

Farbenblum, B., & Berg, L. (2020). 'We might not be citizens but we are still people': Australia's disregard for the human rights of international students during COVID-19. *Australian Journal of Human Rights, 26*(3), 486–506.

Finestra, C., McFadzean, D., & Williams, M. (1991–1999). *Home improvement.* ABC.

Gomes, C. (2010). Active remembering in utopia. In O. Guntarik (Ed.), *Narratives of community: Museums and ethnicity* (pp. 290–316). MuseumsEtc.

Gomes, C. (2015). *Multiculturalism through the lens: A guide to ethnic and migrant anxieties in Singapore.* Ethos Books.

Gomes, C. (2017). *Transient mobility and middle class identity: Media and migration in Australia and Singapore.* Palgrave Macmillan.

Gomes, C. (2018). *Siloed diversity: Transnational migration, digital media and social networks.* Palgrave Pivot.

Gomes, C. (2022). *Parallel societies of international students in Australia: Connections, disconnections and a global pandemic.* Routledge.

Gomes, C., Chang, S., Jacka, L., Coulter, D., Alzougool, B., & Constantinidis, D. (2015, December 1–4). *Myth Busting stereotypes: The connections, disconnections and benefits of international student social networks* [Conference presentation]. The 26th ISANA International Education Conference Melbourne, Victoria. https://isana.proceedings.com.au/docs/2015/FullPaper-Catherine_Gomes.pdf

Gomes, C., Hendry, N., DeSouza, R., Richardson, I., Hjorth, L., Harris, H., & Coombs, G. (2021). Higher degree students (HDR) during COVID-19: Disrupted routines, uncertain futures, and active strategies of resilience and belonging. *Journal of International Students, 11*(S2), 19–37.

Green, E. (2023, April 26). *More Australians turning off meat as inflation rises.* News. Com. https://www.news.com.au/finance/money/costs/more-australians-turning-off-meat-as-inflation-rises/news-story/5ada620614aa6c5622bd01980677e54e

Hong, L., & Huang, J. (2008). *The scripting of a national history: Singapore and its pasts.* National University of Singapore Press in conjunction with Hong Kong University Press.

International Organization for Migration. (2023). *Migration data portal.* United Nations Migration. https://www.migrationdataportal.org/themes/international-students.

Kang, K. (Developer). (2021–present). *Doogie Kameāloha, M.D* [TV series]. Disney+.

Khoo, E. (Director). (2001). *One leg kicking.* MediaCorp Raintree Pictures.

Khoo, G. C. (2009). Reading The films of independent filmmaker Yasmin Ahmad: Cosmopolitanism, Sufi Islam and Malay subjectivity. In D. P. S. Goh, M. Gabrielpillai, P. Holden, & G. C. Khoo (Eds.), *Race and multiculturalism in Malaysia and Singapore* (pp. 107–123). Routledge, Taylor & Francis Group, Milton Park, Abingdon, Oxon.

Khoo, G. C. (2011). Taking liberties: Independent filmmakers representing the tudung in Malaysia. In A. Weinberg (Ed.), *Islam and popular culture in Indonesia and Malaysia.* Routledge.

Khoo, T. L. (2003). *Banana bending: Asian-Australian and Asian-Canadian literatures.* Hong Kong University Press.

Lloyd, J., & Croft, D. (Creators) (1972–1985). *Are you being served?* [TV series]. BBC.

Lo, J., Chan, D., & Khoo, T. (2008). Asian Australia and Asian America: Making transnational connections. *Amerasia Journal, 36*(2), xiii–xxx.

Lorre, C., & Aronsohn, L. (Creators). (2003–2015). *Two and a half men* [TV series]. Warner Bros. Television.

Marchetti, G. (1994). *Romance and the 'yellow peril': Race, sex and discursive strategies in Hollywood fiction.* University of California Press.

Pereira, A. A. (2015). *Singapore chronicles – Eurasians.* Straits Times Press.

Qi, J., & Ma, C. (2021). Australia's crisis responses during COVID-19: The case of international students. *Journal of International Students, 11*(S2), 94–111.

Roddenberry, G. (Creator). (1987–1994). *Star trek: The next generation.* Paramount.

Russo, F., & Barnsley, W. (2022, May 9). *Why farmers are dumping truckloads of avocados despite massive food price rises.* Channel 7 News. https://7news.com.au/lifestyle/personal-finance/why-farmers-are-dumping-truckloads-of-avocados-despite-massive-food-price-rises-c-6731991

Sanders, R. (Director). (2017). *Ghost in the shell*. Paramount Pictures.

Sardana, S. (Creator). (2001–2006). *The Kumars at no. 42* [TV series]. BBC.

Simmonds, C. (2017). *Act of translation* [Theatre production]. Act of Translation.

Tan, K. P. (2009). Racial stereotypes in Singapore films: Commercial value and critical Possibilities. In D. P. S. Goh, M. Gabrielpillai, P. Holden, & G. C. Khoo (Eds.), *Race and multiculturalism in Malaysia and Singapore* (pp. 124–140). Routledge.

Teo, A., Wee, T. S., Tan, S., & Loh, A. (Creators). (1995–2003). *Under one roof* [TV series]. MediCorp.

Teo, S. (1997). *Hong Kong cinema: The extra dimensions*. British Film Institute.

Tran, L., & Gomes, C. (2015). *Stereotyping international students is unjust*. University World News, (00371). http://www.universityworldnews.com/article.php?story=20150428141315340

Tran, L. T., & Gomes, C. (2017). Student mobility, connectedness and identity. In L. T. Tran & C. Gomes (Eds.), *International student connectedness and identity* (pp. 1–11). Springer.

Walliams, D., & Lucas, M. (Creators). (2003–2006). *Little Britain* [TV series]. BBC.

4 Communicating with international students and why this matters

Introduction

A few years ago, I excitedly presented my latest research on international students at a conference on multiculturalism. My data – which was collected that year and involved talking to 60 international students – was part of a bigger project looking at the everyday lives of temporary migrants. It also included working holidaymakers (backpackers) and knowledge workers on work visas. During my presentation, I talked about my participants revealing how they barely, if ever, watch or listen to the media in Australia. I pointed out that while there is a public broadcaster dedicated to culturally and linguistically diverse (CALD) communities who are often migrants from non-English-speaking backgrounds, my participants never engaged with this broadcaster despite being available on the internet, radio, and television. Known as the Special Broadcasting Corporation or more popularly as SBS, this broadcaster was created by the Australian Government in 1980 to specifically cater to migrant audiences.[1]

SBS's role in assisting migrants from CALD communities to feel a sense of belonging in their adopted country where they are citizens or permanent residents has been fundamental, particularly before the advent of the internet. Today, digital media is ubiquitous in everyday life, and, hence, migrants with access to Wi-Fi and sometimes a virtual private network (VPN) – whether permanent and part of the citizenry or temporary – have the ability to access media productions from anywhere in the world and at any time. The internet's ability to facilitate a person's reach to almost any media production anywhere in the world, as long as these are online, means migrants may form disassociations with the new home/ host country. During the question-and-answer time of the conference mentioned earlier, a very well-respected scholar who I admired, questioned me about my data. The scholar felt that I was wrong because SBS was specifically developed for migrants and was surprised to learn only 2 out of my 60 participants had actually heard of SBS. I explained that being transient migrants, international students said to me that they barely watched or tuned into Australian media for 2 reasons. The first reason is that international students could peruse the

DOI: 10.4324/9781003547082-5

internet for news and entertainment according to their taste. Often, they watch and listen to news and entertainment programmes (including infotainment) which they are familiar with back in their home countries. Usually, these are American-centric since American media is globally available. The second reason lies in the fact that international students are only transient in the host country. As an undergraduate international student explained to me: 'this is not my country'. Being transient in a host country where cultural, social, and familial ties are non-existent does not make for investments even when they involve media consumption. I agree that media catered to CALD communities provides a cultural anchor in the adopted country that migrants now regard as home. However, study destinations are transient with the concept of home being ephemeral.[2] Clearly, international students are not engaging with the host country even when there are broadcast mediums specifically designed for migrants from countries which are culturally and linguistically different from the host country. The same, moreover, can be said about international students and their engagement with digital platforms and host country-based digital content. While the digital is the primary space for communicating with international students (e.g. education providers using the digital space for curriculum and pedagogy), this does not necessarily mean that international students are regularly, actively engaged in the host country's digital environment.

By focusing on the topic of well-being, this chapter reflects on a suite of questions to argue that communication with international students is crucial for their well-being since this impacts their transient migrant experience in the host country. So how do we communicate with international students about their well-being? Do international students know how to find information on taking care of themselves in the host country? Are the ways in which we communicate with the citizenry effective in communicating with international students? Since international students are digitally savvy and mostly occupy the same digital communication worlds and use the same digital platforms as the host country community, shouldn't communicating with them be easy? Why does communicating with international students the 'right way' matter?

Why international student well-being matters

As mentioned in the introduction of this book, the quality of life for international students as transient migrants has become just as important as the course experience (Forbes-Mewett, 2019; Marginson, 2014; Marginson et al., 2010; Tran & Dempsey, 2017). Before the COVID-19 global pandemic, there was increasing scholarship calling for a more holistic understanding of the international student experience, which is not solely steeped in the study experience but includes the non-study lived experiences of students (Gomes, 2022; Phan et al., 2019; Tarzia et al., 2019–2022). These scholars suggest that the lived experiences of international students – including accessibility

to goods and services, employment and employability, self-perceived identities, social and cultural cohesion, aspirations, and media/communication
use – are key tenets of international student well-being and directly correlate with the ways students engage with their courses. Emerging academic
discourse on the impact of the global pandemic on international students
in Australia and elsewhere has concentrated specifically on economic and
financial losses (Hurley, 2020), international student future enrolment and
mobility (Qi & Ma, 2021), student rights and well-being (Farbenblum &
Berg, 2020; Gomes et al., 2021), and speculating on the recovery and future of international education (Hurley, 2020). What the research has *not*
addressed, however, is whether student support services in international
education destinations are able to keep up with the evolving international
student experience and thus provide suitable well-being support to match
students' needs. The scale and impact of COVID-19 on international students
are unmatched with no historical template to understand if institutions and
student support services truly understand the lived experiences of students
whose education, expectations, aspirations, and daily lives have been left
with unending uncertainties. In Australia, for example, media and industry
reports point to the difficulties new international students face particularly
in securing suitable accommodation for the duration of their study. This is
because of a number of related factors colliding in Australia, such as the lack
of available rental properties in the housing market particularly in and around
campuses, and the very high cost of rental properties themselves (Shams,
2023). The result is homelessness, couch surfing, overcrowded apartments,
and hot bedding where students share the same bed with others (Fulloon,
2023).[3] Moreover, the high cost of living in Australia due to (post) pandemic
inflation, supply chain issues, and uncertainty in the employment sector of
suitable jobs has not only impacted citizens in Australia but also international students (Wijaya, 2023). This is because international students often
take up casual jobs in industries such as hospitality and retail, which many
of them lost due to COVID-19 pandemic restrictions. Looking for alterna-
tive employment opportunities in order to sustain themselves, international
students turned to gig economy platform work in the transport and delivery
sectors as ride-share drivers, and food and grocery couriers. Gig economy
platform work is attractive primarily because of its ease of entry (e.g. lack
of need for formal qualifications other than a driver's license or almost no
waiting time) and flexibility of work hours (Chou & Gomes, 2023). To afford
an Australian education, some international students take up loans from their
home countries, and thus depend on their casual jobs to assist them with loan
repayments (Forbes-Mewett et al., 2009), thus resulting in students taking on
too much casual work, worrying about their financial situation, or most likely
both.[4] The ongoing impacts of the COVID-19 pandemic have clearly placed
student well-being as central to the international student experience and thus
transient migrant experience.

While this chapter acknowledges how important international student well-being is, the focus is on how we communicate with them. Here I argue that the ways in which the host country communicates with international students are crucial for their well-being and thus their study and transient migrant experiences. There has been a significant amount of work on how settler migrants communicate with each other and create a sense of home and belonging in their adopted countries through digital communication technologies (Baldassar et al., 2023; Cabalquinto & Zhao, 2023; Wilding & Winarnita, 2022) as well as how transient migrants (e.g. international students, knowledge workers, working holidaymakers/backpackers, forced migrants) use these technologies for similar reasons (Gomes, 2017, 2018). Such work is important because digital communication technologies including social media platforms have, since the early years of the new millennium, become vital for settler migrants in creating a home for themselves while still keeping cultural and societal links with the country of birth. For transient migrants, digital technologies help plug the gap physical distance creates between themselves and loved ones back home, while keeping them connected with transient subjects similar to them who they may depend on as sources of information. This is because international students see each other as trustworthy sources of information primarily because of their shared experiences as foreign students.

There is also now increasing attention paid to how host countries communicate with migrants, particularly from CALD backgrounds. This has led government departments, media companies, non-government organisations (NGOs), not-for-profit organisations, and commercial entities with stakeholder interest in CALD communities to develop well-being programmes specifically for migrants. For instance, there are NGOs and not-for-profit organisations specifically dedicated to helping vulnerable new migrants, such as asylum seekers and refugees, settle in Australia by assisting them with housing and employment. There is also an increased awareness by these stakeholders that there needs to be cultural knowledge when communicating well-being topics which otherwise may not be discussed or taboo for migrants, such as those pertaining to mental health and domestic abuse. Host countries thus have become much more aware of their increasingly multicultural and, therefore, multilingual growing population that stakeholders steadfastly translate information into key migrant languages. The key problem, however, is whether the information is on the target migrants' radar and thus being successfully communicated to them.

Being host to almost a million enrolled international students just at the cusp of the COVID-19 pandemic, Australia clearly requires solid programmes aimed at international student well-being. Australia first started attracting international students as far back as 1951 through the Colombo Plan (Gomes, 2015; Kent, 2020). The Colombo Plan was an education and training programme which saw soon to be decolonised nations and former colonies of the British

Commonwealth sending their students to the United Kingdom and to the other Western developed countries of Australia, Canada, and New Zealand in the Commonwealth of Nations. These students were trained in skills that would assist in the economic, infrastructural, and social (e.g. medical and dental) development of the countries they come from through sponsorship from the Colombo Plan programme which took the form of scholarships and bursaries (Gomes, 2015; Kent, 2020). By the 1980s, Australia became a global player in the export of education in the region, by offering courses and qualifications which attracted students almost resoundingly from Southeast Asia and, increasingly, from Northeast and South Asia. Seeing how popular Australian education was becoming particularly in the Asian region due to Australia's geographical proximity to the region, the Australian Government decided to start charging international students 'full fees' for their education.[5] Before the COVID-19 pandemic, international education brought in AUD$37.6 billion (Binsted, 2023).[6] For perspective, this is an increase of AUD$21.3 billion from the end of 2013 when international education brought in AUD$16.3 billion through full-fee paying international students. By full fees, international students pay sometimes 4–6 times more for their education than domestic students (Tran & Gomes, 2017). Moreover, outside education providers, there are international student stakeholders, such as accommodation providers, that benefit from high numbers of international students. The result is a robust and high in demand rental market. This is because international students live in purpose-built accommodation in close proximity to their institution's campus. This proximity is preferred particularly in Australian cities because of safety and accessibility. Approximately 90% of Australia's international students study with education providers in state capitals (Hurley, 2020).

While Australia is also host to international students enrolled in high schools, they only represent over 2% of the international student cohort in Australia with over 50% enrolled in universities as undergraduate and postgraduate students (Department of Education, 2023). Undergraduate international students largely fund their education in Australia through private means. In other words, they or their families pay for their education and living expenses. Increasingly, international students may take up loans from banks in their home countries to fund their education. Postgraduate students undertaking research degrees such as PhDs and Masters by Research might be funded by scholarships from their home nations with a few funded by the Australian Government. This includes the Department of Foreign Affairs' Australia Awards scholarships and the Department of Education's Research Training Program International Fee Offset Scholarships (Department of Education, 2024; Department of Foreign Affairs and Trade, 2024). By the end of 2019, there were 956,773 international students enrolled in education institutions throughout Australia (Department of Education, 2020). With that said, Australia has graduated millions of international students since the late 1980s when full fees for international students were introduced. Clearly, full-fee education has not negatively impacted the international education sector in Australia. To its credit however, Australia recognises that the increasing numbers of international students means a duty of care to the well-being of the hundreds of thousands of international students enrolled in education institutions throughout the country. The significance of international student well-being is seen in the formation of networks and organisations dedicated to not only international student well-being but to the advocacy of student well-being.

In the late 1980s, the international student-led National Liaison Committee for International Students (NLC) was formed in order to represent the concerns of all higher education international students in Australia. The reason for the formation of the NLC was the concern that international students – who by now were paying full fees – had no representative body. International students, in other words, realised that paying for their education meant that they were different from domestic students who already were represented by the National Union of Students. Here issues of value for money in the quality of their education together with student well-being, such as anti-racism, became paramount concerns behind NLC's advocating for international students. In 2010, the NLC was then replaced by the Council of International Students Australia (CISA) as the peak body representing and advocating for international students in Australia.[7] Run by international students on a voluntary basis, CISA liaises with international education stakeholders – including federal and state governments – on international student concerns and issues.[8]

In 1989, 4 years after the Australian Government started introducing full fees for international students (Parliament of Australia, n.d.), the Overseas Student Advisers' Network (OSAN) was formed 'in response to the support needs of the growing number of international students enrolling at Australian Universities' (ISANA, 2024). Now known as ISANA: International Education Association, the network is made up of over '600 members across all education sectors …. draw[ing] from a range of professional groups including academic staff, marketing, recruitment and educational support specialists' (ISANA, 2024). Amongst other activities, ISANA advocates for international student well-being while running professional development programmes to train and educate student services staff about best practice in international student well-being. These include developing resources to help international students take care of their mental well-being such as the 'Lived Experience Toolkit (LET): Mental health support for international students'.[9] The importance of the mental well-being of international students has become paramount that organisations dedicated to mental well-being in Australia such as Orygen – a leading youth mental health charity dedicated to research, education, policy, and clinical care – have developed programmes specific to assisting international students (Orygen, 2020). The issue, however, which these organisations face is the use of their resources amongst international students. Before I discuss projects, I have been involved with, which directly address the communication with international students issue, I would like to highlight why the communication-migrant nexus is a significant area of not only research but of practical use.

Why is communication important for culturally and linguistically diverse (CALD) communities?

In 2022, my colleagues and I undertook a project looking at the uptake of COVID-19 vaccines amongst vulnerable and hard to reach migrant communities in Australia (McKay et al., 2022). Looking at Chinese- and Arabic-speaking migrants in Australia, we found that our participants were not engaging with Australian Government and media resources on vaccines. Instead, the Chinese permanent migrants and international students we interviewed noted that they either turned to Chinese social media for information about COVID-19 information or to other Western sources of information. Specifically, the Chinese permanent residents who had lived in Australia for an average of a decade, almost exclusively engaged with Chinese social media (e.g. WeChat) for their information about vaccines. The reason why they did this was not only because of trust in the Chinese authorities but also because Chinese social media was where they communicated with their loved ones still in China. The Chinese international students, meanwhile, preferred to look to US media to understand about COVID-19 vaccines, noting that they were interested in what Dr Anthony Fauci – the then director of the National Institute of Allergy and Infectious Diseases and the chief medical officer to then President Donald Trump – had to say.

One of the most significant findings of this COVID-19 vaccine uptake project was that translations of government messages and information about the COVID-19 pandemic during the first year of the pandemic into Arabic were not totally in this language but mixed with Parsi. While Arabic and Parsi writing may look similar, they are 2 completely different and distinct languages. Hence, the participants who reported on this translation faux pas assumed that the translation of pandemic messaging and information was done through Google Translate – a generative artificial intelligence (AI) – rather than by a proper human translator. This led to participants feeling confused about the messaging around COVID-19 and vaccines. Besides losing trust in official messaging and information about the pandemic due to poor translations, the concern we had as researchers was the twin issues of trust and trauma. All the Arabic-speaking participants in this particular study had experienced forced migration. In other words, they were at one-time asylum seekers and refugees who came to Australia to escape war and conflict in their countries and regions of birth. Escaping from the traumas of war and conflict, followed closely by the traumas associated with relocation and settlement, our Arabic-speaking participants faced another kind of trauma – that of not knowing what to do during a global health crisis. As former refugees and asylum seekers who experienced hardship at the hands of those in authority in their home countries and regions, followed by challenges caused by Australian policies on forced migrants, such as indefinite asylum-seeker detention, our Arabic-speaking participants felt that they could not trust the Australian Government to provide their communities with the right information about the pandemic. The result was the Arabic-speaking community taking communication matters into their own hands. Here members of the Arabic-speaking community in Australia started translating all pandemic-related information from the Australian Government onto a grassroots-run Facebook group (Min Australia, 2023). While this Facebook group existed before the COVID-19 pandemic, the fact that there was a dedicated social media group for the accurate translation of Australian Government communications is indicative that the Arabic-speaking community felt that there clearly was a need for this service. While the Arabic-speaking community translates official information for their members from trusted sources, thus ensuring accurate and timely communication of messages and news, particularly around well-being, migrant communities may not always circulate the right information to those living in the host country.

In work I conducted with Shanton Chang on international student information-seeking behaviours (Chang & Gomes, 2017a, 2017b), we showed that international students lack awareness of where to find information which assists with their well-being. Specifically looking at international students' knowledge of who to call when faced with critical incidents where life and property are threatened, we found that students did not engage with basic information widely known to the citizenry. For instance, the number/s to call in an emergency (i.e. police, ambulance, health services). This is because international students almost always live in an information bubble often made up of international students from their home countries (Gomes et al., 2015). Thus, when international students seek information on not only critical incidents but more widely on taking care of their well-being, they do so by relying on fellow international students who know as much as them (Gomes et al., 2015).[10]

Not knowing who to call when something bad happens became a reality for a 19-year-old Chinese international student studying in Melbourne. On April 15, 2016, Jeremy Hu and his friends – who were also Chinese international students – met in an alleyway with another group of Chinese international students in a dispute over a girl. In China, disputes like these are not uncommon where a show of force with an entourage is more performance of strength rather than intention to harm (Lee, 2018). However, the result of this confrontation was Jeremy being assaulted. Instead of seeking medical help, both groups of Chinese students took Jeremy to a nearby hotel to rest up. The following morning, Jeremy's condition worsened and the students finally drove him to a hospital, but did not leave their names. Jeremy passed away a week later with medical professionals noting that if he had been admitted immediately, he would not have died. The international students with Jeremy did not know what to do to look after Jeremy's well-being. Part of not knowing what to do may have been informed by the students fear of getting into trouble with the police (Younger, 2018) and/or being deported back to China (Gomes et al., 2022). Jeremy's companions and assailants, in other words, lived in a silo and therefore an echo chamber occupied by fellow Chinese international students who knew as much as each other on what to do and who to call.

Silos and echo chambers

In previous work, I recognised that international students in Australia live in silos with other international students, particularly their co-nationals (Gomes, 2018). International students, in other words, inhabit both 'physical and online silos or bubbles which make social cohesion with the larger community in the receiver nation difficult, if not impossible' (Gomes, 2018, p. 72). Living in these silos means that international students not only remain attached to other members of the silo they are in but also in some degree trapped in them as well. Living within a silo may be useful in terms of connecting with others who are similar. This can assist international students adjust to living, studying, and even working in an unfamiliar country in the short run. However, in the long run, silos are not especially beneficial for international students and the wider destination site community. Being in friendships, associations, and communities made up solely of international students and reflective of their key identities both however means that students – particularly if they come from the same country – exist in echo chambers. By living in echo chambers, individuals and groups do not allow themselves to be exposed to information (e.g. news and opinions) outside these friendships, associations, and communities.

Living in an echo chamber means that people surround themselves with others (in the physical and in the digital world) who resonate and thus reinforce the same identities, values, ideologies, opinions, and assumptions (Karlsen et al., 2017) without alternate perspectives other than their own. In the survey of 6,699 international students in Australia, my colleagues and I found a correlation between the information-seeking behaviour of international students and their friendship groups (Gomes et al., 2013). International students who were only friends with international student co-nationals were limited in their information sources as compared to international students who were friends with international students who were not co-nationals. International students who had domestic students in their social networks were, in turn, exposed to an even larger pool of information sources than the previous 2 groups. By information sources, I refer to both online sources (e.g. websites and social media) and physical sources (e.g. family, friends, and acquaintances).[11] We found that this was across the board on questions about study, accommodation, health, news, and entertainment. In other words, international students who did not have friends outside their co-national boundaries had limited knowledge of information sources since the same information was circulated and reinforced within the echo chamber. Meanwhile, international students who are friends with local students had wider information sources, such as exposure to news sources, websites, and social media platforms outside those used by co-nationals. For example, Chinese international students with local friends were exposed to different forms of opinions, assumptions, and so on because they were balancing Chinese social media platforms (e.g. Weibo) with non-Chinese social media platforms (e.g. Facebook). Doing so, they were being informed by different perspectives because their trusted sources (their social media contacts) were mixed. Individuals live in echo chambers because they receive information from trusted sources, other international students. For instance, when asked where they get their information about living as international students in Australia, respondents in the survey generally said: 'I get information about NEWS in Australia also from friends and Facebook' and 'Friends, word of mouth'.

This brings us back to the example of the friends and associates of Jeremy Yue who did not know what to do and who to call when faced with a critical incident where life is at stake. Part of the reason why international students may not know what to do is that they are caught in echo chambers where their friends in Australia are co-nationals or other international students from the same country. Hence, what their friends know is primarily the same as what they know. If international students only know other international students from the same country not only as friends but as flat mates, course mates, and workmates, the result would be students living in communal silos based on nationality despite living in an overseas country. These silos thus breed communities of international students who know and experience as much as the next person in that community. This happens not only in the real but also the online environment leading to not only limited information but also misinformation. The information/misinformation is broadcasted and circulated within the silos international students belong to, sometimes for extended periods of time in both environments.

In the survey on international students and their friendship groups, we found that 4% of the 6,699 respondents admitted that they had no friends in Australia. While the percentage may seem small, this group is still a matter of concern. This is not only because of the perceived loneliness and isolation they face without face-to-face social encounters but also the lack of social networks they have in Australia. While our research did not ask respondents about friendships they may maintain in the digital space (e.g. with the friends from their home nation and/or those made specifically within the digital environment), as researchers our concern was that these international students were not only physically and socially isolated from peers in Australia but also from sources of information which could help with their everyday life and well-being.

In another research project I conducted from 2013 to 2016, international students in Australia told me that often the friends they make which last the entire duration of their time as students are those who they meet for the first time when they arrive. Often these will be established international students they first meet. In some Australian capital cities, international education stakeholders run 'welcome desks' at airports to welcome new students. These welcome desks are manned by international students who provide welcome packs as well as information for new students. Likewise at some institutions, established international students such as second- and third-year undergraduates assist with mentoring new international students, particularly in first-year orientation programmes. These first-year students then take up the mantle of their seniors and become mentors and orientation leaders themselves. This ensures the silos continue despite the well-meaning intentions of assisting new students adjust.

While these trusted sources may provide reinforcement of our identities, values, ideologies, opinions, and assumptions, they also become sources which have limited perspectives. However, even more of a concern is that these echo chambers are subject to misinformation. In the digital age, this misinformation spreads quickly by becoming viral.[12] Let's take the example of employment for international students where students enter the gig economy as delivery platform workers, often as food delivery couriers, sometimes almost immediately when they first come to Australia.

International students turn to the gig economy, as noted earlier in this chapter, because of the flexibility of work hours, which allows them to work around their studies. With the gig economy, there is also an ease of entry due to the lack of employers in the traditional sense thus facilitating students to work almost immediately without going through any job application process. This also means that international students who are only allowed to officially work for 48 hours per fortnight during semester times due to visa restrictions are able to work beyond this. Meanwhile, recently graduated international students are on visas allowing them to live, work, as well as study in Australia for between 18 months and 4 years so as to gain work experience and to fill Australian skill shortage gaps. During the COVID-19 pandemic, international students who lost their jobs working casual positions as waiting staff in food outlets (e.g. cafes and restaurants) turned to delivery driving as an option for income to pay for their living expenses. Food delivery is thus undertaken primarily for financial sustenance with no professional or future residency benefits.

The lack of policies governing the rights and safety of international students as food delivery workers has opened the door for a plethora of unregulated online sites targeting current and future students with general to specific information on undertaking platform food delivery work. While some of the sites are grassroots initiatives where students themselves aim to educate and inform fellow international students about best practice as food delivery workers (e.g. Punjabi social media influencer F.M. Jalad), other online sites appear to be anonymous with no definable affiliation (e.g. Overseas Studies Guide to Study in Australia 2020). However, what these unregulated and grassroots information sites have in common is that they directly and primarily speak to international students searching for guaranteed employment alternatives through the food delivery (and rideshare) gig economy. These sites are interpreted as identifiable, acceptable, and trusted sources of information by international students in need of work so as to fund their living in Australia. These sites, unfortunately, do not let students know about the dangers associated with gig economy work. For instance, international students taking up food delivery courier work are sometimes unaware of basic road and safety rules and their rights working in the gig economy. Seeing the need for road safety programmes in 2020, the Victorian State government funded a training package aimed specifically at international students and delivered by a Swinburne University consortium on road safety, courier well-being, and legal rights (Swinburne University of Technology, 2020).[13]

Using the digital to engage with international students – getting it right

The advent of the COVID-19 pandemic, however, forced education providers in Australia and elsewhere to pay closer attention to how they engage with not only international students but also domestic students. Here the digital campus became the primary way in which students and staff engaged with each other in both the teaching and learning spaces as well as the student support space. A digital campus quite simply is the official online location of institutions where staff and students engage with each other. Here teaching and learning activities are conducted not only through learning management systems but also through institutional social media channels, websites, emails, digital tools such as mobile applications, webinars, digital protocols, and institutionally related channels of communication (Chang & Gomes, 2022). Digital thus includes being online and the technologies and electronic processes used to facilitate this. Going almost completely online and thus immersed in the digital environment/space meant that institutions have been engaging with students of all levels (e.g. vocational, undergraduate, postgraduate) studying remotely, interstate, or overseas in the range of key student services of health, safety, and well-being (including counselling services, chaplaincy, and LGBTIQ+ support), academic skills (including research, library, reading, writing, and language), careers and employability, and financial and legal support. However, for digital campuses to work effectively, they need to be welcoming and inclusive to allow for the diversity of students to participate. This is because there is the potential for digital segmentation if students and student support staff (e.g. professional administrative support services) choose to use their own digital experiences (e.g. cultural perspective, preferences, and biases) to interact and engage with each other.

While education providers in Australia and elsewhere already have some form of digital engagement with students as part of their bespoke digital campus strategy, the pandemic revealed that institutions have not really understood the nuanced digital behaviours of their diverse student body and the capabilities and challenges of their staff (Veerasamy & Ammigan, 2022). This is because staff and students come from different cultural, linguistic, and national backgrounds, leading to a diversity of digital experiences that govern the way people behave in the digital space. To work effectively, digital campuses need to be welcoming and inclusive to allow for the diversity of students to participate. Domestic and international students, for instance, are not homogenous in their digital behaviours but increasingly varied due to differing digital experiences based on country of origin and unequal experience with digital technologies (Chang & Gomes, 2022). Staff and students who were not prepared for complete digital engagement of learning, teaching, and student services during the COVID years were frustrated. Additionally, even before the pandemic, universities in Australia and worldwide have been increasingly pairing with industry partners as a segue for future employment of graduates (Li & Fang, 2019). With remote working becoming the new norm, graduates may well be expected to have key strategic remote working and collaboration skills. Most recently, prominent international education scholars, de Wit and Jones (2022), critiqued the governmental and higher education institutional focus on traditional physical mobility and Western centrism in international education. They point to the need to explore the impacts of digitalisation in higher education as a part of understanding international education in the higher education space. This means that higher education providers will have to continue to evolve and improve their digital engagement offerings since they service a diversity of students made up of international and domestic students.

Successful staff-student engagement in non-pedagogical student services helps build community and belonging within an institution, assists with student learning, and enhances the overall student experience (Hughes, 2021; Mohamed et al., 2021). Building successful student service environments in digital campuses, however, is reliant on effective engagement with students – both domestic and international. Recognising the importance of higher education institutions' services and engagement in supporting students (Marginson et al., 2010) to provide strategies and approaches for higher education providers to successfully engage with students through digital campuses.

Conclusion

Australia is one of the only countries in the global international education sector where international students are provided with work rights while studying (Last, 2023). Hence, international students not only study and live in and around where their institutions are located but also work in local cafes, eateries, retail shops, and shopfronts, and increasingly as food delivery riders and rideshare drivers. Despite being an integral part of the ethnographic landscape of the places they occupy, as the previous chapters have also shown, international students are arguably not an integrated part of the wider community. To remedy this, international students have found ways to explore and communicate their experiences as transient migrants in Australia. The following concluding chapter brings the ideas put forward in this book by suggesting that international students create roles for themselves in Australian society and presents a list of policy and practice implications which can be used not only in Australia but in countries with growing international education sectors.

Notes

1 While SBS features programmes from overseas in the language they were made in, it also translates locally made English-language programmes into the multiple languages spoken and understood by the myriad of migrants in Australia. On its website, SBS explains its role as:

[Reflecting and exploring] the evolving diversity of Australia, investing in initiatives to deepen its connections with communities, sharing their stories and giving a voice to those often unheard, with the aim of increasing understanding and respect of the differences that make up society today. Its content, services and engagement with communities help enable all Australians to feel included and to contribute to Australia's prosperity. SBS is a truly distinctive network, showcasing multicultural, multilingual and First Nations stories otherwise untold in the Australian media.

Special Broadcasting Corporation (2024b)

SBS sees its role in Australia's multicultural community as facilitating all Australians 'regardless of geography, age, cultural background or language skills, should have access to high quality, independent, culturally-relevant Australian media, and be able to participate in public life' (Special Broadcasting Corporation, 2024a).

2 For instance, international students would be living in rental apartments or houses with flatmates for a limited time. Both their accommodation and flatmates sometimes may last anywhere from a few weeks to a few months to a few years depending on how long students' courses last. When I was an international student in Melbourne undertaking a PhD, I moved 8 times. The shortest time I was in at a premises was a week because I felt unsafe. Some of my flatmates did not last for more than a night because the place I was renting was used as a stop over for people looking for quick accommodation.

3 Education providers in Australia are located in and around city and CBD areas in both state and regional capitals. Properties in these areas are highly sought after due to proximity to work and amenities.

4 This situation also takes please in other countries such as Canada and New Zealand. See, for instance, Calder et al. (2006) for the Canadian example and Beban and Trueman (2018) for the New Zealand example.

5 Australia's capital cities are key international education destinations and only a few flying hours away from major Asian cities. For example, Western Australia's capital city of Perth, which is home to state universities such as the University of Western Australia, Curtin University, and Murdoch University, is only 4 hours 45 minutes away from the Indonesian capital of Jakarta and 5 hours away from Singapore and 5 hours 45 minutes to the Malaysian capital of Kuala Lumpur.

6 This figure represents the years 2018–2019 while in 2019 2020 this amount decreased to AUD$37.4 billion due to the COVID-19 pandemic when international education halted student mobility.

7 The NLC lost credibility in 2009 because it was taken over by a Chinese-Australian businessman known as Master Shang who used the organisation to further his own business agenda (Gilmore, 2009).

8 On its LinkedIn page, CISA states the following as their key activities:

Advocate for the interests and needs of international students; •Advocate for high quality education for international students; •Facilitate network building among stakeholders with an interest in supporting international students; •Host an annual national forum for international students; •Provide a means of consulting and engaging with international students; •Host future international student roundtable events in partnership with various government entities; •Promote cross-cultural awareness and interactions in Australia; •Advocate for non-racist, non-discriminatory law reform concerning international students.

Council of International Students Australia (2023)

9 See https://www.letyourstorytalk.com/ (Let Your Story Talk, 2022).

10 Moreover, international students may look for information on their well-being from online sources they are familiar with – often this means reverting back to the familiarity of the home country (Alzougool et al., 2013). A case in point was during the devastating 2011 earthquake in Christchurch where some international students, while trapped under rubble, used their smartphones to call their families back home for help rather than the New Zealand emergency services. This is because they did not know who to call for help in New Zealand.

11 Sometimes the online and physical environments may overlap. For instance, contacting a family member through digital communication platforms such as email and/or social media.

12 During the COVID-19 pandemic, for instance, the amount of misinformation and disinformation about the virus and COVID-19 vaccines led to unrest worldwide, particularly in the West, the site of heightened conspiracy theories leading to open protests in the streets. Protesters were unhappy with pandemic restrictions, mask mandates, and compulsory vaccinations. Protesters felt that pandemic restrictions and mask mandates were an overreach by governments as some believed the virus was made-up and that compulsory COVID-19 vaccinations were against their human rights.

13 The consortium is made up of Fit2Drive Foitsundation, D'Accord Occupational Assistance Services, and JobWatch.

References

Alzougool, B., Chang, S., Gomes, C., & Berry, M. (2013). Finding their way around: International students' use of information sources. *Journal of Advanced Management Science*, *1*(1), 43–49. https://doi.org/10.12720/joams.1.1.43-49

Baldassar, L., Stevens, C., Krzyzowski, L., & Jones, B. (2023). Diverse aging and health policy for digital aging futures. In S. I. Rajan (Ed.), *Handbook of aging, health and public policy* (pp. 1–21). Springer. https://doi.org/10.1007/978-981-16-1914-4_88-1

Beban, A., & Trueman, N. (2018). Student workers: The unequal load of paid and unpaid work in the neoliberal university. *New Zealand Sociology, 33*(2), 99–131.

Binsted, S. (2023, October 11). *International student statistics Australia 2024*. Finder. https://www.finder.com.au/international-money-transfers/international-student-statistics

Cabalquinto, E. C., & Zhao, X. (2023). A (dis)connected homescape: The promise, limits, and paradox of migrants' homemaking practices in the digital age. In P. Boccagni (Ed.), *Handbook on home and migration* (1st ed., pp. 388–398). Edward Elgar Publishing.

Calder, M. J., Richter, S., Mao, Y., Kovacs Burns, K., Mogale, R. S., & Danko, M. (2006). International students attending Canadian universities: Their experiences with housing, finances, and other issues. *Canadian Journal of Higher Education, 46*(2), 92–110. https://doi.org/10.47678/cjhe.v46i2.184585

Chang, S., & Gomes, C. (2017a). Digital journeys: A perspective on understanding the digital experiences of international students. *Journal of International Students, 7*(2), 347–466. https://doi.org/10.32674/jis.v7i2.385

Chang, S., & Gomes, C. (2017b). International student identity and the digital environment. In I. Steglitz & B. Kappler (Eds.), *Learning across cultures: Locally and globally* (pp. 39–62). NAFSA: Association of International Educators.

Chang, S., & Gomes, C. (2022). Why the digitalization of international education matters. *Journal of Studies in International Education, 26*(2), 119–127. https://doi.org/10.1177/10283153221095163

Chou, M.-H., & Gomes, C. (2023). Politics of on-demand food delivery: Policy design and the power of algorithms. *Review of Policy Research, 40*, 646–664. https://doi.org/10.1111/ropr.12543

Council of International Students Australia. (2023). *Council of International Students Australia*. LinkedIn. https://www.linkedin.com/company/cisa-national/about

Department of Education. (2020). *International student data 2019*. International Education Data and Research. Australian Government Department of Education. https://internationaleducation.gov.au/research/International-Student-Data/Pages/InternationalStudentData2019.aspx

Department of Education. (2023). *International Student Data – full year data (based on data finalised in December 2022*. International Education Data and Research. Australian Government Department of Education. https://www.education.gov.au/international-education-data-and-research/resources/international-student-data-full-year-data-based-data-finalised-december-2022

Department of Education. (2024). *Research training program*. Australian Government Department of Education. https://www.education.gov.au/research-block-grants/research-training-program

Department of Foreign Affairs and Trade. (2024). *Australia awards*. Australian Government Department of Foreign Affairs and Trade. https://www.dfat.gov.au/people-to-people/australia-awards

de Wit, H., & Jones, E. (2022). A missed opportunity and limited vision for internationalization. *International Higher Education, 109*, 5–6. https://ejournals.bc.edu/index.php/ihe/article/view/14471

Farbenblum, B., & Berg, L. (2020, June 30). *International students and wage theft in Australia*. SSRN. http://dx.doi.org/10.2139/ssrn.3663837

Forbes-Mewett, H. (2019). Mental health and IS: Issues, challenges and effective practice. *Research digest*, Vol. 15, International Education Association of Australia. https://ieaa.org.au/common/Uploaded%20files/Research%20Publications/2019/PUB-IEAA-Mental-Health-and-International-Students-Research-Digest-15.pdf

Forbes-Mewett, H., Marginson, S., Nyland, C., Sawir, E., & Ramia, G. (2009). Australian University international student finances. *Higher Education Policy, 22*(2), 141–161. https://doi.org/10.1057/hep.2008.4

Fulloon, S. (2023, June 30). *Hot-bedding: This student is sharing a bed with a stranger.* SBS News. https://www.sbs.com.au/news/article/this-student-is-sharing-a-bed-with-a-stranger-because-she-cant-afford-the-rent/vi26387yj

Gilmore, H. (2009, May 9). Overseas student group at centre of bullying claims. *Sydney Morning Herald.* https://www.smh.com.au/national/overseas-student-group-at-centre-of-bullying-claims-20090508-axzz.html

Gomes (2015). Negotiating everyday life in Australia: Unpacking the parallel society inhabited by Asian international students through their social networks and entertainment media use. *Journal of Youth Studies, 18*(4), 515–536. https://doi.org/10.1080/13676261.2014.992316

Gomes, C. (2017). *Transient mobility and middle class identity: Media and migration in Australia and Singapore.* Palgrave Macmillan.

Gomes, C. (2018). *Siloed diversity: Transnational migration, digital media and social networks.* Palgrave Macmillan.

Gomes, C. (2022). *Parallel societies of international students in Australia: Connections, disconnections and a global pandemic.* Routledge.

Gomes, C., Berry, M., Alzougool, B., & Chang, S. (2013). Home away from home: International students and their identity-based social networks in Australia. *Journal of International Students, 4*(1), 2–15.

Gomes, C., Chang, S., Jacka, L., Coulter, D., Alzougool, B., & Constantinidis, D. (2015). Myth Busting Stereotypes: The Connections, Disconnections and Benefits of International Student Social Networks. *The 26th ISANA International Education Conference was held in Melbourne, Victoria,* 1–4 December at the Pullman on the Park. http://2016.isanaconference.com/wp-content/uploads/2016/02/Gomes.pdf

Gomes, C., Chang, S., Guy, M., Patrao, F., & He, S. A. (2022). *Contact points: Enabling international students during critical incidents. Revised Edition. Report.* https://www.contactpoints.org/Contact%20Points%20Report%202022%20update%20v10.pdf

Gomes, C., Hendry, N. A., De Souza, R., Hjorth, L., Richardson, I., Harris, D., & Coombs, G. (2021). Higher degree students (HDR) during COVID-19: Disrupted routines, uncertain futures, and active strategies of resilience and belonging. *Journal Of International Students, 11*(S2), 19–37. https://doi.org/10.32674/jis.v11iS2.3552

Hughes, H. (2021). Connected transitioning communities for international students via social media. In S. Chang & C. Gomes (Eds.), *Digital experiences of international students: Challenging assumptions and rethinking engagement* (Vol. 2020, pp. 151–173). Routledge.

Hurley, P. (2020). *Issues paper: International students vital to coronavirus recovery.* Mitchell Institute. https://www.vu.edu.au/sites/default/files/issues-brief-international-students-covid.pdf

ISANA. (2024). *About ISANA.* ISANA: International Education Association Inc. https://isana.org.au/home/about/

Jalad, F. M. (2022, October 20). *50$per hour? Food delivery job Australia.* YouTube. https://www.bing.com/videos/search?q=youtube+food+courier+work+australia&&view=detail&mid=8CAC4B8FDA93D8C682A08CAC4B8FDA93D8C682A0&&FORM=VRDGAR&ru=%2Fvideos%2Fsearch%3Fq%3Dyoutube%2Bfood%2Bcourier%2Bwork%2Baustralia%26FORM%3DHDRSC6

Karlsen, R., Steen-Johnsen, K., Wollebæk, D., & Enjolras, B. (2017). Echo chamber and trench warfare dynamics in online debates. *European Journal of Communication, 32*(3), 257–273. https://doi.org/10.1177/0267323117695734

Kent, A. (2020). Overseas students coordinating committees – The origins of student support in Australia. *Transitions: Journal of Transient Migration, 4*(1), 99–114. https://doi.org/10.1386/tjtm_00015_1

Last, F. (2023, May 4). *Work while studying abroad: 6 countries where it's ok.* GoAbroad.com. https://www.goabroad.com/articles/study-abroad/can-you-work-while-studying-abroad#:~:text=6%20countries%20that%20allow%20international%20students%20to%20work,5.%20Germany%20...%206%206.%20United%20Kingdom%20

Lee, J. (2018, March 15). *Death of Jeremy Hu highlights 'moral obligation' to protect international students.* ABC News. https://www.abc.net.au/news/2018-03-15/death-highlights-obligation-to-protect-international-students/9538860

Let Your Story Talk. (2022). *Lived Experience Toolkit: Mental health support for international students.* https://www.letyourstorytalk.com/

Li, R., & Fang, W. (2019). University-industry-government relations of the ministry of industry and information technology (MIIT) universities: The perspective of the mutual information. *PLoS ONE, 14*(2), e0211939.

Marginson, S. (2014). Student self-formation in international education. *Journal of Studies in International Education, 18*(1), 6–22.

Marginson, S., Nyland, C., Sawir, E., & Forbes-Mewett, H. (2010). *International student security.* Cambridge University Press.

McKay, D., Naghizade, E., Zhao, F., Yang, X., Aburghif, H., Arrad, D., Buchanan, G., Low, E., Astall, E., & Chang, S. (2022). *Vaccine information needs of the Chinese and Arabic communities in Australia: An investigation and partial solution.* Australian Digital Health Agency.

Min Australia. ‫.من آستراليا‬ (2023). Facebook. https://www.facebook.com/Min.Australia/

Mohamed, N., Schoen, S., Yu, X., & Kappler, B. (2021). Creating an online orientation course: The journey to internationalizing the campus. In S. Chang & C. Gomes (Eds.), *Digital experiences of international students: Challenging assumptions and rethinking engagement* (pp. 174–192). Routledge.

Orygen. (2020). *International students and their mental health and physical safety. Report.* https://www.orygen.org.au/Orygen-Institute/Policy-Areas/Employment-and-education/Education/International-students-and-their-mental-health-and/International-Student-Mental-Health-and-Physical-S?ext=

Parliament of Australia. (n.d.). *A brief history of education reform. Higher education report.* https://www.aph.gov.au/Parliamentary_Business/Committees/Senate/Education_and_Employment/Higher_Education/~/media/Committees/eet_ctte/Higher_Education/report/c02.pdf

Phan, H., Le, T., Tran, L. T., & Blackmore, J. (2019). Internationalization, student engagement, and global graduates: A comparative study of Vietnamese and Australian students' experience. *Journal of Studies in International Education, 23*(1), 171–189.

Qi, J., & Ma, C. (2021). Australia's crisis responses during COVID-19: The case of international students. *Journal of International Students, 11*(S2), 94–111.

Robinson, T., Robinson, R. N. S., & Hoffstaedter, G. (2023). Seeking justice beyond the platform economy: Migrant workers navigating precarious lives. *A sustainable tourism workforce.* Routledge. pp. 92–109.

Shams, H. (2023, February 11). Thousands of international students set to return to Australia amid rental crisis after China online learning ban. *ABC News*. https://www.abc.net.au/news/2023-02-11/international-students-forced-back-to-study-sydney/101958984

Special Broadcasting Corporation. (2024a). *Our history*. SBS. https://www.sbs.com.au/aboutus/who-we-are/our-history/

Special Broadcasting Corporation. (2024b). *Why we exist*. SBS. https://www.sbs.com.au/aboutus/who-we-are/why-we-exist/

Swinburne University of Technology. (2020). *Food delivery work: A guide for international students*. https://commons.swinburne.edu.au/file/00480a84-4495-4e39-9711-57f92d736a02/1/food_delivery_work-transcript.pdf

Tarzia, L., Forbes-Mewett, H., Tran, L., Seagrave, M., Humphreys, C. F., & Murdolo, A. (2019–2022). *International student' sexual and intimate partner violence experiences study*. Australian Research Council Discovery Project Grant.

Tran, L., & Dempsey, K. (2017). *Internationalization in vocational education and training: Transnational perspectives*. Springer.

Tran, L., & Gomes, C. (2017). Student mobility, connectedness and identity. In L. Tran & C. Gomes (Eds.), *International student connectedness and identity: transnational and trans-disciplinary perspectives* (pp. 1–11). Springer.

Veerasamy, Y. S., & Ammigan, R. (2022). Reimagining the delivery of international student services during a global pandemic: A case study in the United States. *Journal of Studies in International Education, 26*(2), 145–164. https://doi.org/10.1177/10283153211052779

Wijaya, S. (2023, February 18). *International students are back, but they're struggling with Australia's rising cost of living*. ABC News. https://www.abc.net.au/news/2023-02-18/treatment-for-international-students-after-covid/101964512

Wilding, R., & Winarnita, M. (2022). Affect, creativity and migrant belonging (vol 15, p. 283). *Communication, Culture & Critique, 15*(4), 555. https://doi.org/10.1093/ccc/tcac027

Younger, E. (2018, April 30). *Shengliang Wan jailed for killing Chinese student Jeremy Hu in Melbourne alleyway*. ABC News. https://www.abc.net.au/news/2018-04-30/shengliang-wan-sentenced-for-killing-jeremy-hu/9710100

Next steps

Introduction

This book reports and reflects on more than a decade of interviews with international students and observations of the international education sector in Australia. Australia is a key international education hub which has successfully sold education as a commodity for almost 40 years. International education and its secondary industries such as building, rental and accommodation, tourism, retail, and hospitality are key Australian exports servicing students from around the world who travel, live, study, and work in this country. International education has expanded to include transnational education where education providers set up offshore campuses in a scenario where the education destination comes to the student and not the other way around. Nonetheless, international travel by students themselves is still more favoured. As this book points out in various places, a degree from a reputable overseas Western institution has social cache.[1]

While international students in Australia are visible actors in institutions of learning, they are also visible and active participants in the broader Australian community where they live and work. International students create roles outside of education so as to navigate their transient migrant experience. They are able to do this because of Australia's position as an international education hub across an ecology of education sectors where Australian capital cities are transformed into international student cities, and provisions such as work rights are accorded to overseas students. The chapters in this book thus capture the lived experiences of international students as they navigate through the dynamic challenges and transformations international education has afforded them. This book presents readers with 2 takeaways: (a) that the international student experience is filled with twists and turns in terms of everyday practices and aspirations, which the COVID-19 pandemic highlighted and (b) that international students develop ways of dealing with these twists and turns organically and creatively despite being transient migrants.

While this book features international students in Australia, the Australian case study presents useful opportunities for policy and practice not only for Australia but for countries wishing to expand their international education sector.

DOI: 10.4324/9781003547082-6

Implications

Rethinking the international student experience and focusing on international student well-being

International education stakeholders – which include government and education providers – charged with the international student experience need to understand that the international student experience is not confined to learning in classrooms. Instead experiences outside the classroom define the international student experience. Hence, international student well-being should not be confined to study but to non-study-related experiences.

Regulating the international student well-being industry

Countries such as Australia have a sophisticated international student well-being industry. This industry is run by government and private entities in both institutional and non-institutional spaces, such as in the case of student accommodation. However, this industry is largely unregulated. Regulating the international student well-being industry means that a good holistic international student experience benefits not only international students but also the reputation of destination sites.

Rethink how we protect international students who work while studying

Increasingly international students are taking up part-time work in destination sites which provide them with work rights. These student workers who make contributions to destination country communities do so as service providers and to the country as a whole as taxpayers. Such contributions mean that certain employment protections must be put in place to protect the transient migrant student.

Important to understand how local communities navigate attitudes and treatment of international students

International students have been the subject of political, economic, policy, academic, and media discourses concerning education, migration, population control, and finance. However, understanding how local communities in destination sites feel about international students and establishing programmes which allow international students and local communities to engage with each other becomes essential in cultivating a positive experience not only for international students but the local communities they are part of and contribute to.

Researchers should be open to new frameworks for analysing
the international student experience since cohorts change due to
policy amendments and practical considerations

For instance, during the COVID-19 pandemic in 2021, the Australian Government allowed international students to work unlimited hours in certain industries needing workers but reversed this decision in 2023 (Heffernan, 2023). Prior to COVID-19, international students were able to work for 40 hours per fortnight. At the time of writing, regardless of which industry they are employed by, international students are able to work in Australia for 48 hours per fortnight during semester times. They are, however, able to work unlimited hours during non-semester periods. International student work rights have, unfortunately, led to some people from overseas enrolling in Australian institutions in order to work rather than function as genuine students (Dhawan, 2024). Such a scenario means that researchers need to use flexibility when understanding the diversity of international students and their experiences. One size, in other words, does not fit all.

Note

1 Sometimes a degree from an offshore institution may not carry the same weight as a degree from the home country of that institution. At other times, studying remotely from an overseas institution may make the qualification worthless. For instance, in early 2023, the Chinese Government made the decision not to accept overseas degrees of Chinese students who were not physically in the countries of their institutions. This is because, from early 2020 to early 2023, countries outside of China were offering international students online access to courses for students who were not able to travel due to COVID-19 pandemic restrictions (Xing et al., 2023).

References

Dhawan, S. (2024). Australia cracks down on international students looking to work rather than study - Investing Abroad News. *The Financial Express*, 3 April. https://www.financialexpress.com/business/investing-abroad-australia-cracks-down-on-international-students-looking-to-work-rather-than-study-3444982/

Heffernan, M. (2023, July 4). 'Need to work': International students brace for restricted working hours. *The Sydney Morning Herald*. https://www.smh.com.au/education/need-to-work-international-students-brace-for-restricted-working-hours-20230703-p5dlb9.html

Xing, D., Boscaini, J., & Terzon, E. (2023). *Students rush back to Australia after China bans online learning with foreign universities.* ABC News. https://www.abc.net.au/news/2023-01-31/chinese-students-australia-return-university-online-class-ban/101906794

Index

Note: Page numbers followed by "n" refer to notes

Act of Translation 47, 56, 59–61, 64n5
America Calling: A Foreign Student in a Country of Possibility 49
anti-racism 72
Are You Being Served? 59
Army Daze (1996) 52
artificial intelligence (AI) 50, 73
Asian-Australians 43
Asian Australian Studies Research Network (AASRN) 51
Australia 3; COVID-19 pandemic and 6–8, 16n2; degree courses in English language 9; education sector as an ecology 41; graduate employment. 11; high cost of living in 69; as international student country. 8–12, 86; international students in 3–6, 20; international student 'welcome desks' at 11–12; job market and 9; lack of rental properties in housing market in 69; local communities navigate attitudes and treatment of international students 87; new frameworks for analysing international student experience 88; permanent residency in 11; PhD degree in 23, 26; proximity 9; qualitative research with international students 12–15; quality of education in 9; reasons to study in 8–10; regulating international student well-being 87; rethinking and focusing on international student well-being 87; rethinking to protect international students who work while studying 87; as safe, friendly, and multicultural 10;

undergraduate international students in 7, 71; warranty requirement for first year international student 6–7; *see also* Melbourne CBD
Australian banks 11
Australian Catholic University 37
Australian cultural traits 60
Australian Government Research Training Program (RTP) scholarship 8
Australian life, integral part of 20–22
Australian media, international students and 67–68
Australian post-study visa policy 40
Australians from Latin America 43
Australian Tax Office Website 45n6
Australian Trade and Investment Commission (AUSTRADE) 10
Australian Universities Accord Interim Report 21

Bhandari, R. 49
Billionaire Saverin 44
Breakfast at Tiffany's 53

Caucasians viii
Chan, D. 51
ChatGPT 50
Chieng, R. 47
Chinese-Malay-Indian-Others (CMIO) racial framework 52
Chinese social media 73
Colombo Plan (1951) 70–71
Council of International Students Australia (CISA) 72, 81n8
COVID-19 pandemic ix; casual work due to 69; fees increase due to 71;

high cost of living in Australia due to 69; international education recovery after 55; and international student 6–8, 16n2, 22, 26–27; international students before 68–69; Melbourne CBD before 37–38, 39; movement restrictions during 28; racism and xenophobia due to restrictions during 30; scale and impact of 69; unemployment due to 69; vaccine uptake project 73–75
Crazy Rich Asians 53
culturally and linguistically diverse (CALD) communities 52, 67
cultural shock viii, 7

Deng Xiaoping 54
Department of Education's Research Training Program International Fee Offset Scholarships 71
Department of Foreign Affairs' Australia Awards scholarships 71
digital campus strategy 78–79
digital communication technologies 70

education fees, by international students 20–21, 38–39
ELICOS Association of Australia, 16n1
embody transience, international students 25–27
Emo of Friesland 1
employment, international students and 56
English as foreign language 9–10
English Language Intensive Courses for Overseas Students (ELICOS) 2, 21

Facebook 74, 76
Fauci, A. 73
food delivery couriering in Australia 40
Forbes-Mewett, H. 49
Fu Manchu 52
funding 71

Ghost in the Shell 53
global mobility, student's 1–2, 5–6
Goodness Gracious Me 54
Google 10
Google Scholar 29
Google Translate 73
Greek-Australians 43

Higher Education Contribution Scheme (HECS) 41
Home Improvement 59
Hong Kong cinema 53

international education ix; recovery after COVID-19 55
International Education and Skills Strategic Framework ix
International Education Association (ISANA) 72
international education recruitment agencies 19
International English Language Testing System (IELTS) 2–3
International Organization for Migration 20
international student mobility: literature on 4–5; scholarships and 5
international students ix; appeal of an 4–6; are visible actors in institutions of learning 86; in Australia 3–6, 20; Australian media and 67–68; as backdoor migrants 42; case study 74–75, 86; as casual workers 21–22, 32n8; challenges faced by 22; communicating with 67–79; communication through digital communication technologies 70; conventionalising in public discourse 48–50; before COVID-19 68–69; COVID-19 pandemic and 6–8, 16n2, 22, 26–27; creative canvas and multiculturalism 50–54; cross-cultural relationships 56–57; education fees by 20–21, 38–39; embody transience 25–27; employment and 56; ethnic and gender stereotypes 54; experiences in 2010 54–55; experiences of 47–61; fiction and non-fiction projects on 49; as food delivery workers 77–78; full fees for 72–73; funding by 71; gig economy and 77; as global cosmopolitans 24–25; importance of well-being 68–73; independent living in Australia and 8; integral part of Australian life 20–22; Latin American 39–40; life as an 6–8; part-time jobs by 32n7; perception about 40–44; permanent migrant(ion) frameworks 30–31, 33n10; as permanent residency hunters 3, 42; as privileged foreigners 40;

profit-making education providers and 21, 31–32n2, 44n1; provide labour and services as casual workers 3; racism and 43; reasons for becoming casual workers 22; relying on each other 27–28; in rental apartments 80n2; rethinking about experience of 30–31; scale and impact of COVID-19 on 69; scholarship and 49; significance of 56–57; silos and echo chambers 75–78; social and cultural spaces in real and virtual world 19; stereotyping 42–43; as temporary migrants 19–20, 31n1, 33n9; and their friendship groups 76–77; as transient migrants 22–25, 27; using digital to engage with 78–79; as villain and victim 48–50
international *vs.* domestic student's education fees 38–39
Italian-Australians 43

job creation 30
job insecurity 30
JobKeeper Payment scheme 45n6
JobSeeker 45n6
Johansson, S. 53
Journal of International Students (JIS) 28–30

Khoo, Tseen 51

Larcombe, W. 28
Latin American international students 39–40
LGBTIQ+ 60
Limitless Humans: How Running Helped Me Live a Meaningful Life 49
Little Britain 59
Lived Experience Toolkit (LET): Mental health support for international students 72
Lo, Jacqueline 51

Malaysia viii
Marginson, S. 49
Melbourne CBD 36–44; accommodation in 38, 44n4; cost of living in 2022 41; before COVID-19 pandemic 37–38, 39; during COVID-19 pandemic 41–42; international students and

37–38; international students as food couriers 39; international students at cafes and restaurants 37; overview of 36–37; for Vietnamese international students 41; work in 38–40
Michelle Chong 43
Michelle Yeoh 53
Microsoft 10
Morrison, S. 6, 16n5
multiculturalism 30
Multiculturalism Through the Lens: A Guide to Ethnic and Migrant Anxieties 51–52

National Council for Australia-China Relations (NFACR) xi
National Institute of Allergy and Infectious Diseases 73
National Liaison Committee for International Students (NLC) 72
New Zealand 3
The Noose 43
North America 3

Ommelanden Benedictine monastery 1
One Leg Kicking (2001) 52
overseas education: lead to job opportunities in home country 5; social currency and 5
Overseas Student Advisers' Network (OSAN) 72
O-week festivities 12
Oxford Blues 49

permanent migrant(ion) frameworks 30–31, 33n10
permanent residency in Australia 11

qualitative research with international students 12–15; enabling international students during critical incidents 14; investigating barriers to vaccine uptake 14–15; lived experiences of international students: pivoting on a pandemic 14; mapping identities and networks 12–13; relationship between social roles and information access and use of international students 13–14

Quan, Ke Huy 53
Queensland's University of the
   Sunshine 37

racism 30
Refuge of Hope 39
resource sustainability 30
RMIT University 37
road safety programmes (2020) 78
Roddenberry, G. 50
Ronny Chieng: International Student 47,
   56, 57–59

Sawir, E. 49
scholarships: to international students
   by Singapore government 63n3; to
   international students in Australia 49
Scimago 29
Seinfeld 59
sexual identity 60
*Siloed Diversity: Transnational
   Migration, Digital Media and Social
   Networks* 60
silos and echo chambers 75–78
Singapore viii; multicultural identity
   63n1; scholarships to international
   students.by government of 63n3
Singh, Sukant Suki 49
social currency 9
social media 24
Special Broadcasting Corporation (SBS)
   67; role in CALD communities
   67–68

Star Trek series 50
*Star Trek: The Next Generation
   (TNG)* 50
Swinburne University 78

Tan, K. P. 51
temporary migrants: international
   students as 19–20, 31n1, 33n9;
   vs. transient migrants 22–25
Terminator 50
Thatcher, M. 53
transnational identities 3
Two and a Half Men 59

Under One Roof 53
United Kingdom 3
United Kingdom and Hollywood sitcoms
   see specific sitcoms
University of Melbourne 37
University of Oxford 1
University of Paris 1

vaccinations 81n12
Victoria University 37
Vietnamese international students 23–24
virtual private network (VPN) 67
vocational education and training (VET)
   institutes 21

WeChat 73
Weibo 76

xenophobia 4, 30

For Product Safety Concerns and Information please contact our EU
representative GPSR@taylorandfrancis.com
Taylor & Francis Verlag GmbH, Kaufingerstraße 24, 80331 München, Germany

www.ingramcontent.com/pod-product-compliance
Lightning Source LLC
Chambersburg PA
CBHW071056280326
41928CB00050B/2528